Praise for

MW01089413

In Megan Bacigalupo's *In the Cobwebs of My Mind*, the author pulls open the curtain and gives us a rare glimpse into an incredibly multidimensional and multifaceted experience, one that changed her life forever. That this eclectic soul was able to remember the juxtaposed visions and hallucinations is our gift, for we are now much more than a visitor stepping into her ICU and glaring at her with fearful eyes.

–Tim Miejan, editor of The Edge (1996–2020)

Megan captures her story in a blend of her real survivor journey, coupled with the power of her imagination in a magical world she's created. I have reviewed many authors, but this book stands in a class of its own. This is the most unique story of its genre I have read.

—Kim Jefferson Justus, Host on Brain Injury Radio Network, Author and Photographer

Imagine hopping on your bike one day and in the next moment you are tasked with mending a vast black hole in the multiverse? ... You awaken in your hospital bed to be told that you have a subarachnoid ruptured brain hemorrhage, you are given a task...

—Jane Evershed, Artist, Muralist, Author, Writer, Art Teacher

The fact that in this book Megan imaginatively charts her healing journey through a magical exploration of several artistic disciplines is nothing short of miraculous. What a ride. Sail on, Silver Girl!

—Bain Boehlke, Founder and Founding Artistic Director of The Jungle Theater, Minneapolis Minnesota

I find Megan's works to be in touch with what we find on the edge of our consciousness in our everyday lives. Her style is insightful and sometimes very bold. She is an individualist and a free thinker. An excellent read.

[This book] is grand and magical, taking you on a journey deep into her mind and personal experiences. It brings to light the indescribable event that others sometimes do not understand!

Anyone who has had a brain aneurysm or is close to someone who has will be well served by reading this book.

Thank you, Megan, for continuing to raise awareness for others, and wishing you all the success in doing this.

This book will help teach and educate people and families that have been through this ordeal and more importantly survived. Megan's story is incredible, remarkable, and miraculous not only because it is true but it will help people heal.

Three people close to me have had or had aneurysms and [Megan] was so lovely to spend time giving me resources and knowledge from experience so that I could be of service to them in their healing process. Her gift with words is amazing considering all she has been through.

In the Cobwebs of My Mind

Wisdom
Editions
Minneapolis

FIRST CALUMET EDITION 2023
In the Cobwebs of My Mind: A Vivid and Magical Recollection of Surviving a Brain Hemorrhage
Copyright © 2023 by Megan Bacigalupo. All rights reserved.

10 9 8 7 6 5 4 3 2 1
ISBN: 978-1-960250-87-2

Cover and interior design: Gary Lindberg

In the Cobwebs of My Mind

A Vivid and Magical Recollection of
Surviving a Brain Hemorrhage

Megan Bacigalupo

Minneapolis

Table of Contents

This book is dedicated to Savona and Jordyn O'Leary
and to Andrea, their mother and my sister,
who left this earth in 2004.

Introduction

I would have never imagined in my wildest dreams that in 2017, I would have a sudden and spontaneous ruptured brain aneurysm. Not only did I survive the stroke, but I came out of the whole ordeal walking and talking. I was mysteriously spared on so many levels. So it has become my wish to provide hope to brain injury survivors and to those closest to them. My story reveals the strength of an injured and healing brain. Beating or cheating death, call it what you will. In this writing, I explore the resilient nature of the human mind and all that it witnessed in its struggle to survive. My story was developed with much evolution as my injured brain was healing and, to my surprise, creating. It conjured many things. This was written in no specific order, in a discombobulated form, much like my brain after it suffered its injury. It changed along with the art and the images. It became rich. It became vivid and theatrical. Ultimately it is a survivor story, but it is no ordinary hospital story. I wrote this book for many reasons, and this book has a mind of its own. Yet it seemed to line up as part of a mathematical equation in its own peculiar way. I learned to push my brain and use parts of it that I didn't know existed. I developed a new rhythm in my thinking patterns that seemed to occur only after the injury. I learned to trust it, although it seemed foreign. I hope that my story will encourage all brain injury survivors to tell their stories however they wish to. We all have a story to tell. Perseverance and discipline, combined with determination and grit, were sure things for me. This was especially difficult in the aftermath of a brain hemorrhage. I took my time. There were no rules. I was graced by surprises that I'm beyond grateful for. This recollection is a tale of how a routine bike ride home from work became the wildest ride of my life.

A vision inspired me to write a play, and when the play was written, it immediately began to change shape and form. It was born to run and become, become all and anything that it wished to. This book is the result of that process. It all started with a vision that I had to follow. It summoned me. It has led me in the most healing and therapeutic way.

It took me to so many places and surprised me all along. It is still surprising me to this day. My vision was given as a way for me to climb past surviving into new dimensions, which resulted in storytelling. This project has taken many twists and turns, never stopping and in constant motion. It kept calling me back to move again. A moving entity with many pieces. It is gestalt. It is a puzzle. It moves together and yet is always open to reshaping, leaving it in a perpetual state of becoming. It originated in my core self. I tapped into the deep layers of my soul. I went into the back alleyways of my mind. What was born in these places surprised me! I think about my first days home out of the intensive care unit. I could not read or concentrate. As a result of my brain bleeding, I had a cut in my field of vision. An area where my brain was damaged created this. It prevented me from seeing clearly. I have a trick eye that I have learned to live with. My headaches were unbearable in the early days of recovery. I vomited easily. My strength was diminished. Sitting on the edge of a chair and bending over to put on my socks was a daunting task. This act alone left me completely exhausted. The confusion inside my injured brain brought me to a place of complete frustration. My once healthy brain was now suddenly pulling, reaching for things that once sat in the forefront of my mind. I had to slowly adapt to my new brain. It was no friend of mine. No one else could see inside this newfound reality. My friends would say things like, "you seem fine." They had no idea how difficult my life had become. When I returned home from the ICU, I kept my head on ice packs most of the day for several weeks. I wondered if I could go on any longer with the head pain that was constant. I had staples in my scalp where a hole was drilled into my skull so that a tube could be inserted into a ventricle in my brain. On a cloudy day, I could not look out the window because it was too bright. Everything was a blur. I never thought I would be where I am today. I am one of the lucky ones. There is hope. I assure you.

Part One:
Early Formations

"You can be cautious, or you can
be creative, but there's no such
thing as a cautious creative."

—George Lois, American Art
Director, Designer, and Author

Magical Muses and My Dual Self/ Getting the Ball Rolling

My muses were chosen, or they chose me long before I suffered and survived a brain hemorrhage. An aneurysm formed and ruptured inside my brain without warning. I had a spontaneous hemorrhagic stroke. The hemorrhage took place in the space inside my brain called the Subarachnoid Space. This type of hemorrhage is referred to in the medical community as SAH. *The subarachnoid space exists between the arachnoid matter externally and the pia matter internally. A network of delicate connective tissues called trabecular connects the two layers and gives this space its characteristic spider web appearance.*[1]

A sly muse is a spider, busy as a trickster. Spider got my attention to research and develop her

---

1   www.ncbi.nlm.nih.gov

as a character along with an ancient god that she hand-picked to accompany her. Spider (the writer's totem) and Nabu (a Babylonian god of writing) entered my life a few years before my medical crisis. Spider began spinning a story in her web long before I was propelled into action to spin mine. It all started when I began getting mysterious spider bites. I had a bad reaction to the venom. This is why I began my research on spiders in 2014. I was writing a story around the same time. It was a story about Mick Jagger (another muse) as a modern-day pantheon god. I was excited about the work I was doing, but I only got so far when writer's block set in. Spider and Nabu never materialized in 2014. They were in a deep slumber. They were sleeping in my notebook and in the documents on my laptop computer. Then several years later, in 2018, about a year after my brain hemorrhage, they came back to life. They had waited patiently to enter this story. They knew the hour of their birth, which was now. They have helped me write, form, and complete this project. These characters are prophetic. They have guided me and given me a tale to write. This is a story of survival. It is a semi-deconstructed and reconstructed story mixed with vivid imagination and mythical magic. I combined my personal story with my medical records and research. It took two tracks: the events that actually happened and the creative development and process that followed. This life-changing, near-death experience led me on an endless journey. It raised my vibrational level to a higher frequency as I entered into higher realms and places of other dimensions. For this, I rejoice.

I had been writing for a little holistic publication, *The Edge*, since 2012. In 2018, I wrote an article about surviving my ruptured brain aneurysm called "In the Cobwebs of My Mind."

> *My body became a clock. Time pushed forward as a force moved me to get me to where I needed to go. I felt like a Derby horse with blinders, and all I could see was the ambulance that I imagined, a life source after it was called.*
>
> *Everything lined up for me almost mathematically on the night of September 20, 2017. This was the night I almost died. I was on a city bike in uptown Minneapolis, on my way home, when without warning, I suffered from a subarachnoid ruptured brain aneurysm, a brain hemorrhage which is a stroke.*
>
> *I heard a whooshing sound in my ears and realized it was coming from inside my head rather than externally. The wheels of the cars around me were turning in sync with the sound in my head. I went partially deaf and then I jumped off the bike. My vision was getting shaky and blurred.*

*What was to follow was paralyzing pain,
a bomb of a headache in my head and
neck. It was so unbearable I felt myself
detach from it. I was outside my body.
Knowing it was not possible to endure
this pain, I became helpless and had
no choice but to surrender, surrender
to the unknown. I gave up control.*

*In this moment of surrender, a sense of
calm came over me. A force was holding
me. Aware that the clock was ticking
all the while. I guess I was waiting to
be rescued. I was lucky I was in front
of a coffee shop in my neighborhood.
I said to a guy on a cell phone, "Call
me an ambulance." At this point, I was
in shock but still able to function.*

*I handed off the city bike to someone
and a woman sat with me. I heard
the sirens and knew they were for me.
Still in excruciating pain, I answered
the questions the paramedics asked
and they got me in the vehicle. I vomited twice in the ambulance. The next
thing I remember was slowly passing
out. I remember the sensation of being wheeled out of the ambulance,
bouncing, and the rickety noise of the
stretcher as I entered the hospital.*

My medical records state that I arrived unresponsive and moaning. I also learned from my medical records I had a seizure and was repeating to the medical team that I was going blind. I have no recollection of these last details. I was intubated. Two-part surgery. Coiling the ruptured aneurysm by going up into the brain through the main artery in the groin. And a ventriculostomy. Drilling and cutting open a hole in my skull. They inserted a tube or drain to take the pressure off the brain. My blood mixed with my cerebral spinal fluid hung in a bag on my hospital pole... I was attached to it.

I was in the ICU for two weeks.

My angels and the living dead sat, walked, and wandered in a circular motion as they repeatedly passed by my bed with outstretched arms, almost like they were tempting me or inviting me. They each gave me several chances to leave. I continued to watch them. I never felt that I was to join them. They were good company. This was the welcoming committee. They wanted me to know they were there.

Persistent in their motion and very ghost-like, all of them wore hospital gowns like the one I had on. Their faces were all dark and shadowed, without eyes or features. I was trying to figure out who they were. The one who was always sitting had a silhouette of a huge beehive hairdo like the one my grandmother wore for years. She was always in the chair next to me and outstretched her arms from time to time.

I somehow made connections as I traveled in two worlds. I knew they were the living dead and my angels. I stretched in my mind to guess who the others might be. Some were dead relatives, and some were angelic. I would wake up or some nurse would wake me, and my dead relatives and angels would phase out. I had a sense that they were always near, never far away.

In that nanosecond of enlightenment, I knew that the human spirit survives the death of the physical body and I understood that my wandering soul needed to get back into its earthly habitat.

—Janet Bettag[2]

_____

2   *The Edge,* https://bit.ly/3yYiHer

This article was written in my usual style of creative nonfiction and was published by *The Edge* in 2018. Little did I know my story would be published by some of the leading brain aneurysm foundations in the country. First, I contacted The Brain Aneurysm Foundation in Hanover, Massachusetts, the largest private funder of brain aneurysm research in the United States. I was happy that they shared a link to my story. Then I learned of some of the other leading brain aneurysm foundations. All of whom gladly received "Cobwebs" and published it on their social media accounts. Many publications still share my story to this day.

I was particularly lucky to connect with a Facebook group called Brain Aneurysm Survivors. Many of us survivors joked but were completely serious as well about creating a manual to send home with new survivors. We learned so much there. We are honest about what to expect when you first get home… the first year and the second and the third… what the doctors and nurses don't tell you when you are discharged from the hospital. From something so subtle to something huge. You learn firsthand from other survivors. Some survivors are years ahead of you, and then there are the newcomers that just lived through their ordeal. They face the same questions and fears that all of us once faced as we entered into this life-changing experience. There is a real sense of belonging in this group. I'm not one to like groups of any kind. However, I enjoy this particular group for many reasons. It will forever remind me of who I once was, what I survived, how far I have come, and how unbelievably lucky I am. Seeing and hearing the stories of the new survivors fresh out of the hospital with scars and scabs, beaten and bruised. The horror we all faced and lived through. The fear of the new survivors, their questions, anxieties, and insecurities are a refresher. We must never take for granted how far we have come and how many of us were spared. Helping new survivors on their way with a simple comment can help make their day. Brain Aneurysm Survivors Facebook group was an integral part of my recovery. People from all over the world are connected here. My short story, "In the Cobwebs of My Mind," touched the lives of survivors and gave insight to others into what it is like to have a brain injury. Many people emailed me and sent messages via messenger that they had had similar experiences or that a loved one had gone through this experience as well. It is amazing to look back on the reframing of my life that this disastrous, near-death event set in motion.

I remember hearing from a woman in New York City. Her young daughter, Susanna, died from a brain aneurysm. She told me that some of my descriptions of the deceased loved ones that were nearby while I was in the ICU gave her a sense of peace about her daughter's passing. It reassured her that Susanna was in good company as she transitioned from this life to another. It was bittersweet for me to hear from her. The email from Susanna's mother brought me to tears. It moved me deeply. She is a mother, teacher, and writer in Brooklyn, New York City.

Dear Megan,

I just wanted to thank you for your story "In the Cobwebs of my Mind."

My daughter, Susanna, suffered a brain aneurysm four years ago at the age of 5. Since we were traveling by car and she had fallen asleep, we did not know anything was wrong until her heart had already stopped. She was revived and lived until the next day but never woke up again.

I felt that reading your bold description of having a brain aneurysm completed some missing pieces for me. I am also somewhat intuitive, and I believe she did not suffer much pain.

Your candor about being in the comfort of guides, angels, and relatives made me picture Susanna passing peacefully, as I know she did.

Thank you for this important writing. If you plan to write more, I would love to subscribe to your mailing list.

Respectfully,

Trish Freer, Teacher/writer in Brooklyn, NY

After re-reading my short story, *In the Cobwebs of My Mind,* in the first paragraph, I wrote *I felt like a derby horse with blinders.* I realized that I had subconsciously developed and connected with my dual self, *THE HORSE.*

I felt like a derby horse.

I shapeshifted. The horse got me to the hospital fast and helped save my life. This image was a great find in my search for a woman on stage wearing a horsehead. "The Devil's Auction." Female burlesque performer in a horse costume.

I was aware of time being of great importance.
This was all part of my transfiguration. On the
bike and then the horse and shapeshifting.

This image captures the magic that happened.
Photo by Colin Wooderson.

I was riding a bike when my brain aneurysm spontaneously ruptured. I detached myself from the shock and pain as I transfigured into the horse and rider.

These three images tell that well. Then in the final image in this sequence is a woman on a horse with the *Mexican Day of The Dead* costume and her face painted like a sugar skull. I captioned this image…

Almost Dead – Bitter and Sweet

But we made it. This represents the importance of my dual self. We lived. I was starting to die. One summer day, about a year and a half after my incident, I was having a beer at a neighborhood bar. I was re-reading my short story *Cobwebs*. It had just come out in a new publication. Suddenly after reading the first paragraph, I'm sure I had read it dozens of times, it jumped out at me. I saw it in a new and different light. A vision flashed in my mind. It was the opening scene of a play. I saw a powerful image, center stage.

This was an exhilarating moment! I was completely moved. I had an impulse. I had to write a play. I saw a woman standing center stage holding the handlebars of a bike. She had a horse head on her head, and she was wearing horse blinders. This was an abstract and avant-garde image. I became my dual self.

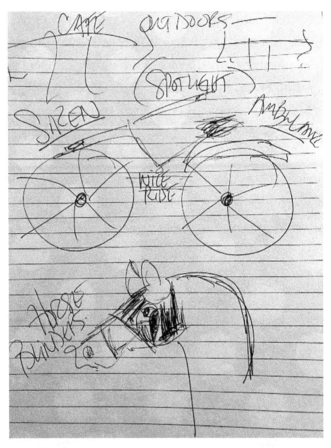

The sketch I did the day I had the vision to write a play.

Shoot for the Stars

Minneapolis, where I live, is a highly saturated "arts" city. As a young person, I worked at the famous Guthrie Theater. I was an usher and an extra in a few shows. Twice, I was in the Charles Dickens classic *A Christmas Carol* and a play called *Double Infidelities*. It was a great experience. Now as a woman in my mid-fifties, after living through the unimaginable and entering into late-onset menopause and all the unbearable symptoms, I wanted to write a play. I had a clear vision, and I needed to go forward. My story was already written. I just needed to turn it into a play. I experimented with a couple of classes; I expected them to teach me how to write a play. It turned out they confused me more than helped me. I enjoy research and I'm rather resourceful, so I began looking at templates and formatting instructions. I thought to hell with it, just start writing. I wrote my play in about six months. It was a grueling process, and I had no idea what I was doing. I had no deadlines or expectations. As I began constructing the play, I was in a race or competition with myself. My brain was still healing, and everything was harder and more stressful and frustrating than it would have been otherwise. It was hard to concentrate and stay focused. Every task I used to take for granted was difficult. I pushed myself. I was pushing myself on all levels. I was working in a restaurant, and I wrote and I wrote. I edited and I edited. I wrote a synopsis and a pitch. The only things that were altered from my real experience were the mythical, fictional characters (Spider, Nabu, and the Horse). I added them into a nonfictional fantasy world that existed in my mind and my memory. I finished writing my play. I was just happy to be done. It was a long shot, for sure. I was well aware of it. It gave me personal satisfaction because, after all, it was what I wanted to accomplish. I was driven to tell this story. My vision was leading me.

Here below is a copy of my original synopsis and pitch that I sent all over the theater community from a large list that was supplied to me. I was hoping to get "Playwrights Week" at the Lark Theater in New York City. I was dreaming big! This did not happen. This is what I sent out to theaters not only in the states but some in England.

My play is about a woman who survived a subarachnoid ruptured brain aneurysm, a hemorrhage, and a stroke. She is a waitress and a writer. The play is about her two-week stay in the ICU. It is in the ICU, in her delirium and drug-induced state, where she meets NABU and SPIDER. NABU: ancient god of writing and wisdom, a scribe, and SPIDER: the writer's totem. This is the first play that I've written. I do not have a writing resume, but I've been a contributing writer for The Edge *magazine since 2012. I sent a link to of my published articles in* The Edge *and my short story* "In the Cobwebs of My Mind."[3]

The purpose of this play is to reach the brain aneurysm communities through writing and art. The story In the Cobwebs of My Mind *first appeared in* The Edge *magazine last summer. It was well received! The foundations are constantly looking for new ways to raise awareness for funding and research. My play is my shot. I am the survivor. My survival instincts and drive*

---
3   https://bit.ly/4097kw2 and https://bit.ly/3FKbBxM,

that got me to the hospital were critical to my survival. This play is a true account of my experience. My experience of surviving the unthinkable.

The god Nabu, the ancient Babylonian god of writing and wisdom; and the spider, the writer's totem, are prophetic. I wrote about them several years before my brain hemorrhage. They were in an entirely different story that was sitting and doing nothing. My characters got to come to life in this play in my brain. Who can think of a better place for a spider (the writer's totem) than in the subarachnoid space of a brain? My brain. A writer's brain.

If you are on the brink of death in the ICU, I think everyone needs a god or goddess working in sync with their totem. My artistic vision is strong. In my original story that was published last summer, I state in the beginning that while waiting for an ambulance, I felt like a derby horse with blinders. It was here that I saw the opening scene of my play. I had a vision after reading that paragraph.

A woman who just jumped off her bike in front of an outdoor café, center stage holding the handlebars of the bike wearing horse blinders, and a horse head, with a clock ticking... and the sound of the ambulance on the way, with the flashing lights. That's when and how I was inspired to write a play. My play is titled *SUBARACHNOID*, which is the place in my brain where my hemorrhage occurred.

I was so full of excitement because of my personal achievements and the fact that I lived to tell this story. I finished what I set out to do while my brain was functioning at a much lower capacity than it ordinarily would have been. Every thought, every sentence, and then moving the thoughts onto paper and then into my laptop computer at a much slower speed. All along, it was stressful to finish. I had ten times more typos than I ordinarily would have had if that is at all possible. My brain hurt and my head hurt. I knew I was pushing myself. I was angry at my brain for not only trying to kill me but for not cooperating with me as I struggled to write my words down and process this story that I was trying to convey as a stage production.

The first thing you learn about your brain after it is injured is that concentration and frustration come at you as you have never known. The stress was mounting daily. This was intense to put my healing brain through so early on in recovery. Some days I would fear having another hemorrhage from stress. I had a love-hate relationship with my new brain. Parts of it were lost and damaged. I am convinced that this project helped my brain become higher functioning at a faster pace by forcing it to work in this capacity. The frustration and the lack of concentration were unbearable. The combination of these two things was extremely painful, also adding memory issues to the list. It was like a tidal wave that kept crashing into me with every step forward. I would be knocked back and down. I fought the waves and stayed afloat.

I not only pushed myself mentally but physically while working in a restaurant at the same time. I wrote the play staying true and stubborn to my vision. I actually thought that someone would be interested in my play. That someone would be impressed not only by the story but the fact that my damaged brain wrote it. These thoughts I processed later, however. I thought it was outlandish and artsy enough to get at least one theater department's attention. So, I had a database of theaters all over the US and from overseas, and I began to pitch my play and submit the material. I wound up with rejection emails and a few sympathy comments of encouragement from those who understood what I had written and accomplished so soon after my traumatic experience. I did have my hopes set on Playwrights Week at the Lark Theater, a play development center in New York City. I was dreaming big and fantasizing. I believed I was going to be chosen.

I would be flown to Manhattan and stay in a hotel that the Lark was paying for in the Hell's Kitchen neighborhood, and they would develop my play with me. I hadn't been to NYC since I was in my thirties. It was fun to research the neighborhood and think about what friend to invite to go with me. My dreams may have been a little too big. But I got over it and came back down to earth. I could stand tall and proud with my printed script in my bag and my pitch letter. Life does go on as they say, or as the saying goes. I would have never guessed what fate had in store for me.

Working with the Master Mentor

My mind was flooded with thoughts and ideas. I was
entering a new classroom that fate had in store for me.

Lo and behold, in the autumn of 2019, I met a theater person. He had alertness and an air about him. He was very present and astute. He seemed to channel energy. He had pillar-like energy. A strong and sturdy figure. He appeared extremely intelligent and interesting. We met at the restaurant I was working in. He told me he was directing a play and gave me a postcard with information about the play and its location. I said oh, I just finished writing a play. He said, "I want to read it." I sent him my play. He told me he was busy with rehearsals and that he would read it when he had time and get back to me. He kept his word. We started meeting on occasion. He told me at our first meeting what he liked about my play. He liked that it took place in other dimensions, and he liked the mythical characters that I introduced. He said he recognized me as a poet and artist. Lastly, he said, you have a story to tell.

He started guiding me. He helped me tap into things that were dormant inside me. He brought me back to my core self. My true creative self. The part of me I hadn't tapped into in a long time. I got back in touch with what was innate and forgotten. One day we met for lunch, and I brought a whole collection of images I had researched on the internet. I had an image, scene for scene, that conveyed what I wanted to express in my show. These images matched what

I had written in my script. I had pictures of the characters and visuals of the set. I thought I was on to a production of some kind. The images helped me imagine what would be taking place on the stage. I showed him my presentation. One image really got his attention.

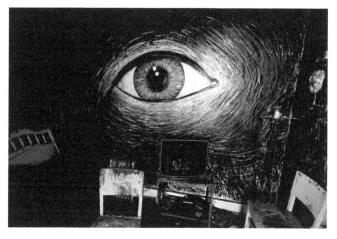

*A still from the film **The Wolf House (La Casa Lobo)** by Cristóbal León & Joaquín Cociña.*

Somehow this image enabled him to visualize what I was trying to show him. He immediately saw what I wanted to create. After viewing these images, he suggested that I start developing a new narrative or production concept that would incorporate these pictures as a new way of telling my story. He also asked me if I could sketch. He saw black and white. Get black paper and a white drawing stick, he said.

He rattled off some words about how he visualized things. His descriptions and ideas were vivid and theatrical. Razor sharp with clarity. I felt an energy shift. An excitement. I had a new vision for my show—a new version and a new vision. A small cast show or, rather, a one-woman show!

Bain Boehlke reading my work (Founder and Founding Artistic Director of the Jungle Theater, Minneapolis, Minnesota).

I was in the habit of mailing or emailing Bain my assignments and work as a follow-up to our meetings. I would always have an assignment. The work that I did under his creative mentoring helped enhance the creative world I was now living in. It was an exciting time for me because my vision was starting to seem real, at least at this moment. Here are some of my reflections on our meetings.

> *I can't get the darkness of a black stage*
> *and actors wearing black out of my*
> *mind with funky projections of white*
> *sketches! With exactly the right light-*
> *ing touch... and almost like a reflector*
> *example a biker that wears a strip of*
> *something that reflects the light...*

> *This is my stream of conscious-*
> *ness... I want it to be funky... I want*
> *this to be arty farty... funky like*
> *Woah... what the fuck was that?*

> *We kind of were building that over*
> *our lunch meeting... to remind you.*
> *A brain hemorrhage, a woman with*
> *a bike, wearing horse blinders....*
> *image to convey ... And then the*
> *sketches to replace the bike, the horse*
> *with blinders with narration... and*
> *all that the brain contains... which*
> *makes the playground for the play...*

*Inside the brain is dark with
the cobwebs projected.*

*My brain is under attack, the imme-
diacy… of the sketches… that you
mentioned while guiding me in the
exercise… you told me to sketch as if I
was in my hospital bed and the only way
to communicate was a piece of chalk
and a blackboard… I like the idea of
two actors wearing all black with light
reflection stripes pantomiming to my
narrative my voice on a prerecorded
microphone—random lines from the
script with all the visuals and sound all
black. The horse, etc… the funky spider
peacock tribal warrior spider and all
the sounds… rolled backdrops of images
I showed you… adaptations… white
chalk sketches projected onto black.*

*I like the quick vision you saw that day
after you saw the eyeball image … the
day that I presented it to you… All the
pictures I found that portray my play…
all the photos I printed from the internet… That's when I saw my vision merge
with your artistic genius… (quickly)
All black stage and wearing black… the
funky music and sounds… Joan Osborne*

and more we haven't discussed music yet… and the freaky hallucinations…

Talk about the original idea formed over our lunch. Where the idea of my voice narration is on the microphone and random actor voices over the microphone… pulling lines from the script of different voices coinciding with actors on stage pantomiming…

Meeting you has helped me remember my dreams and kind of forced me to face my fears at the same time. It's a very spiritual and interesting thing for me to have connected with you I'm sitting on this and hoping that the hands of fate will move…

After he read this, he told me it was cool.

But because of COVID and other obstacles, the play or even the documentary was not going to happen. This is when going forward with the book occurred. The book was first and always going to accompany the play and be sold at each performance. So I decided that the book should be completed first. The next paragraph is the end of my stream-of-consciousness writing that I did when I got home from lunch with my mentor that day.

*My thoughts… The brain is the stage,
and there is trauma and blood in it…
there are lots of medications, hallucinations, and damage… the show should
reflect all of this in the freakiest way
possible, and the sketches are key… my
sketches, thanks to you… for creatively directing me into that process…*

The stage was becoming a reality. I exhausted myself searching for images. Bain and I met about once or twice a month. He would spin off different ideas about the potential of my project. He gave me so much to think about and consider. He would say things like what about a short film?

"You could ask a university student who was in film class to do it as a project," he said. You could film it on your smartphone! He has precision in his voice, that of an instructor. He is an excellent inventor of ideas. His words flow effortlessly with exactness. Or what about a children's book, he said, in a children's hospital, you could have a big picture book. I started imagining this big children's picture book for kids, not a bad idea… with the spider that lived in the brain. It could be in a lobby or a children's area in a hospital. I could visualize kids thinking it was cool to see an illustration of a spider in a brain. Or it could be a picture book, like a scrapbook.

He imagined all sorts of details. This was all on top of it being a book or a one-woman show! He even inspired me to the point of looking into documentary film ideas. So I ventured into online tutorials, free, step-by-step, *How to Make a Documentary Film.* What takes place in documentary filmmaking? Not knowing a thing about documentary filmmaking. He likes to remind me of that. I looked at the different techniques of how things are portrayed. I learned these terms from the internet, pertaining to the making of a documentary film—Actuality, Voiceover, Interview, Archival, Reenactments, Montage Sequence, and Exposition. I started visualizing and imagining all the work and research I had done as a film.

This image inspired me. I started seeing that my work really could become a documentary film. I imagined what it would look like inside a hospital being filmed.

I thought about reconstructing the events. I thought about techniques of distortion and blurring (the indicator to the viewer that the scenes are not real). I pictured all the scenes done this way.

I thought about the exposition. I thought about the dramatic scenes of the incident that would have drawn the viewer in and grabbed their attention. The vivid scenes with the blood and the brain. The horse. How might all of this look in a film? I thought, Fantastic! The raw footage. I could just walk down the street and shoot video images of the coffee shop where I was when I got off the bicycle while experiencing my hemorrhagic stroke.

The Spyhouse in Minneapolis, the coffee shop where I waited for my ambulance on an outdoor chair.

I could interview the staff at the hospital and brain aneurysm survivors in my online group. In the archival parts, I thought about adding the images of my drawings and all the pictures I had found that matched my vision. For the voice-over parts, I would want to use Bain's beautiful speaking voice and his artistic insights into my story. His insights, in combination with his knowledge and artistic skills, would capture the audience without a doubt.

I thought this could be so cool! Ideas flowed so fast, the sounds and images I envisioned for this film. Somewhere in the back of my mind, it all seemed mapped out. I had found images effortlessly that matched my vision. This was a life-changing creative moment for me.

I felt like a creator! I was able to begin expressing myself as I put this work together. I was eager to have it manifest. I was delighted with what my imagination conjured. After almost dying, it was amazing that I could process my experience and create a world inside my healing and damaged brain. I was able to share my experience and somehow tell my story.

*An early sketch of Spider, which seemed
fitting for a children's book.*

I felt like a derby horse with blinders—

my favorite sketch of my dual self.

My sketches of characters I did when the idea
of a children's book entered my mind. Left to
right: Horse, Me, Nabu, and Spider.

Bain's Box

I discovered something about my mentor (Bain Boehlke). I had no idea that this was one of his techniques and how he began his work. I slowly started googling him and researching things about him online. There was a video made for PBS where he talked about dimensionality and how he went about creating his sets. The video presentation went on to say that his creations are real places where the characters live. He does this professionally. I was just doing a day of arts and crafts. However, it did inspire and excite me to be creating something. Looking back on this, I'm sure it was the reason for the box project. It got the wheels of creativity turning.

This photo of my box includes the image of a woman on a bike and a photograph of the coffee shop where I waited for my ambulance.

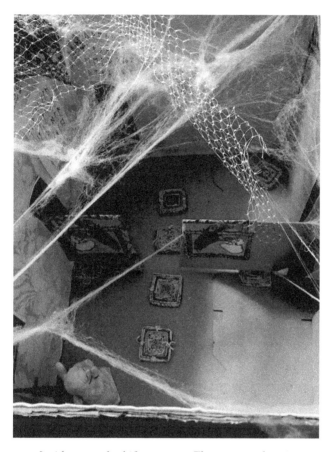

*Inside my makeshift stage set. There was a door in
the middle that represented the portal where the
living and the dead could enter and leave freely,
just as they did while I was in the hospital.*

I felt like I was playing in my old doll house.
It brought me back to the horse barns I made for my
model horses as a kid. I had a dollhouse and model

49

horses, and the horses needed a barn. I began by getting a box from my neighborhood liquor store. I then made a trip to the second-hand store for scraps and bric-a-brac. I bought glue. I started creating the set for my show by setting up a spider web using Halloween stretchy web material. This was the playground for the play (my brain). I even had the dark burgundy fabric for the curtain of a proscenium stage. This was only the first step. I made this box at the same time I was collecting the images. This project sparked creativity. I just went with the flow. I created my box; I hung a couple of the photos on my scrap burgundy curtain. One was a photo of the coffee shop where I waited for the ambulance, and the other was of a woman on a bike. This was the opening scene in the play that my collection of pictures was helping me tell. I also wrote all of the stage visualizations with scene transitions and later found images online to match my ideas. Next was the second homework assignment that my mentor gave me after I made the box of my stage set ideas. He gave me the assignment, to see if I could demonstrate how the scene transitions would happen. Or perhaps show me how difficult it was.

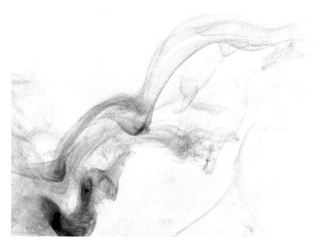

This image represents my blood that burst. I had a brain bleed. A subarachnoid hemorrhage. My brain tried to kill me. It failed. **In the human brain, cerebrospinal fluid is located in the subarachnoid space between the arachnoid mater and the pia matter.**

Homework Assignment/
Scene Transitions

Sliding screen or rolling backdrops for image projections / necessary props.
Use outer stage in front of curtain (small of the stage) for opening scene and final closing scene.

Scene 1: Opening Scene

- Outdoor cafe projected on the curtain (Spyhouse Cafe)

- Large clock ticking audio and visual.

- Girl on bike wearing horse blinkers/blinders/horse head. Holding a bike center stage.

- A guy on a cell phone standing in front of the cafe (After I hand off the bike to him, he exits, wheels bike backstage/offstage)

- Ambulance red flashing lights and sirens

- Barf/vomit bag, vomiting sound over speakers intermingling with siren sound.

- Two actors as paramedics, after taking the vitals scene they help me onto the gurney.

- Lights out. Curtain up.

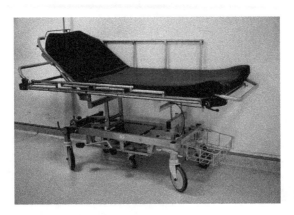

Scene 2: Transition to Inside Hospital / Surgery

When the curtain is up, we see inside the hospital.

Half of the stage is used for the operating room in scene 2. After scene 2, it becomes the busy nurse's station. The other half of the stage is my ICU room. With an open door separating the two for coming and going. Also known as death's door. My character can pass through at any time; visitors come and go through this door. Doctors, nurses and visitors from beyond all use this passageway.

I am lifted onto the operating table and intubated. This operating table becomes the desk and the nurse's station for the rest of the play.

Nabu and Spider are projected on the backstage wall on the screen. This is created for projections. Spider and Nabu's voices are over a microphone, audio coinciding with visual projections.

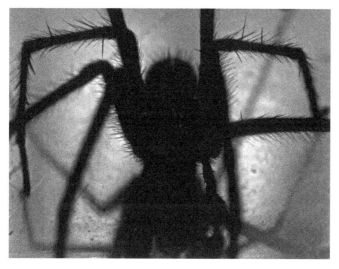

I visualized a projection of a spider for my show. This image captures the look I imagined or desired.

Nabu is a male voice. Spider is a female voice.

Cobwebs and images of the subarachnoid filaments. Coils in a set represent the coils in my brain.

This dramatic image is how I imagined I might look
in a film as I arrived at the hospital unresponsive.

SET – Figure Out Web Net Props

Surgery, audio drilling into my skull, and the visuals
are the letters and numbers that are scattered like the
game of Scrabble on the web. Primordial letters and
alphabets.

Ancient and primordial alphabets.

Coils in the web with blood bags and radiology images of the brain projected during surgery.

Actors: Doctor #1, Nurse #2

Nabu and Spider exit after surgery.

Spider exits beautifully.

Scene 3: I wake up post-surgery in the ICU room

Bathroom in the corner of my room or a door to represent the necessary (duck off and on-stage ability). An IV pole with a tube in my brain attached, and blood bag, and medical vitals equipment. Lots of intermittent beeps that are annoying. Bed and chair next to the bed. Bed tray water in a cup with a straw. Board where nurses chart events when the shift change occurs and a clock on the wall.

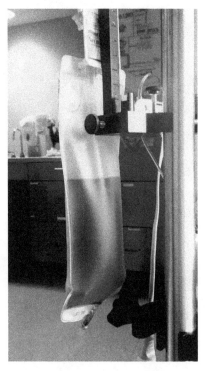

I took this picture from my bed in the ICU.

This is my blood. My blood mixed with my cerebrospinal fluid and hung in a bag on my hospital pole... I was attached to it. It was a very strange realization to know my brain was invaded by a tube to keep me alive. This prevented one of the many complications that can easily end your life—mine was spared.

I was in the ICU for two weeks.

Amazing that in this room so many people visited, both dead and alive.

View from my bed in the ICU. It's hard to believe that so many things took place in this small space. Trees growing, dancing ghosts, and a floating eyeball. In this shot, you do not see the chairs for visitors, the window, and the door.

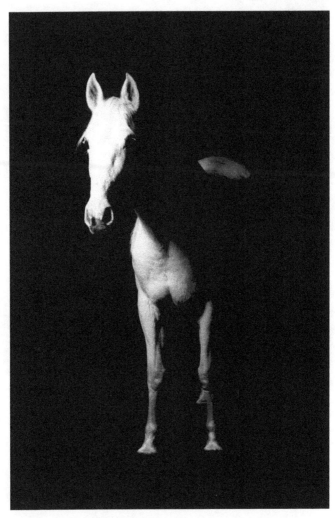

My dual self would pop in to check on my status from time to time. Like a shadow.

I took this photo of my legs in my hospital bed. What did we do before smartphones? I spent two weeks in this position, except for trips to the bathroom and trips in a wheelchair to get brain scans.

Actor 1: Mom

Actor 2 Nora for the wake-up scene.

Actor 3: Nurse

Actor 4: Dan and nurse. After Dan exits.

Actor Doctor, female: Exits after the line "I am your doctor."

Scene 4: Hallucinations, more visitors, tube out of ventricle in brain day

Actor Monica my sister / Actor Colleen my friend / Actor medical student.

I rest after my visitors leave. I wake in the night to an actor (med tech) performing an ultrasound on brain blood vessels.

A resident doctor enters.

Floating blinking eyeball, many online graphics to consider, and perhaps a room full of eyeballs set.

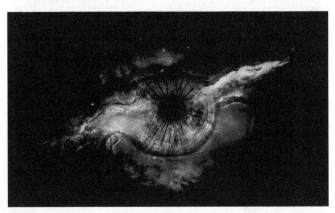

Branches and vines are everywhere and push tree trunk props to coincide with the huge psychedelic hallucinations scene. Projection and prop.

Twirling ghost girl.

Scene 5: Ghost Dance/Nabu and Spider back in the scene

The dancing ghosts, one an angel, and the ghost of my grandmother who sat in a chair next to my bed. All are wearing hospital gowns like the one I had on. Their faces were shadowed, and they were dancing in a rhythmic choreographed kind of way, in a circular motion passing by my bed with outstretched arms, inviting me, tempting me, to cross over to the other world, the famous other side was calling me. These images capture some ghosts rehearsing the dance, not in costume. Not a dress rehearsal.

Spider and Nabu back, microphone voices.

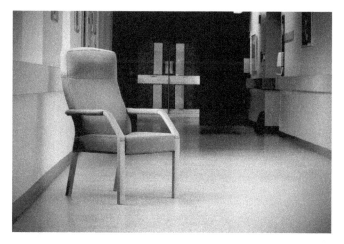

This reminds me of the chair next to my bed in the hospital where my grandmother sat when all of the other ghosts and angels were in the room. I sensed her presence. I was completely aware that it was her. Her face was dark, but her hairdo and her presence gave her up to me. Nonverbal communication...

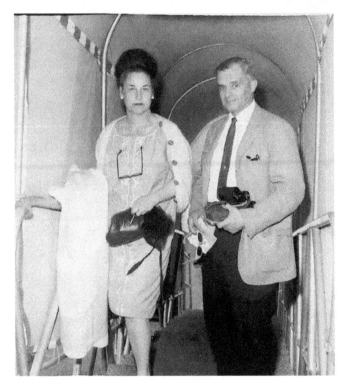

My grandmother. Her signature hairdo
she wore when I was a young girl.

Scene 6: Visit from Ben and Doctors

Ben enters the room and places a book of poetry he wrote on my tray table where we have coffee. We spoke a few words and made strong eye contact. It was soothing. He has beautiful eyes. I remember being so high on medication and tired. He poured the cream into my coffee. He stayed for a bit, and we spoke very little. I had no concept of time while in the intensive care unit. I remember it was comforting to have him near me. A team of a few doctors enters and stands around the foot of my bed. One wears a turban. Lots of doctors from India in neurosurgery. Assessments and test results I felt like a guinea pig that they were studying. I truly was.

Scene 7: Physical Therapist and Counselor / Psychotherapist Department

I passed the walking tests. My behavior towards the psychotherapist department was rude. I have always resisted this unwelcome assessment. I think these types of people should only be sought by the patient and not made available unless desired. She was an unpleasant woman, not quite sure what her title was, but she was trying to help me. I did not like her energy. I had no interest in participating in the psychobabble or her routine rounds of enforcing some kind of case management step. There were times I felt she was judgemental towards me as she was trying to supply resources for me. That was the last thing on my mind. Trying to figure out aftercare. It was premature and protocol for hospital staff. Her energy was bad, and she was giving me a disgusted look.

I decided to insert part of my book proposal here. It is important.

This is very important for all visitors that are not visiting from the other side. This is a message that pertains to all earth-dwelling visitors. It is from the section in my book proposal on comparable titles. I compared three titles. This was the third.

The final and third title I compare is MY STROKE OF INSIGHT: A Brain Scientist's Personal Journey, *written by Jill Bolte Taylor, Ph.D., published by Penguin Books, illustrated edition May 26, 2009.*

Although I'm not a Harvard graduate or a neuroscientist, I can relate to some of the findings in My Stroke of Insight. *She calls it a transporting spiritual experience and the greatest experience of her life. I have to admit I feel the same way about my experience. Taken from* The Harvard Crimson, *the article states that she attained something resembling nirvana. People may ask how something so deadly and traumatic could help you attain nirvana or bliss.*

*At the peak of my subarachnoid rup-
tured brain hemorrhage, a sense of
peace and calm swept over me, and
I knew I was surrendering to a force,
and it was holding me. I was in a mysterious and beautiful place. Same in
my recovery after my headaches went
away. I knew I was on a path to enlightenment, and I had to nurture this
experience and blossom in a new way.
Little did I know. I had to go back in
time to go forward and come around
full circle, which meant facing my fears.
My creativity was alive.* My Stroke of
Insight *talks a lot about the right and
left brain hemispheres and functions. It
was a combination of my left and right
brain working in synchronicity that
developed and brought my story to life.
Jill Bolte Taylor says, "All it takes is a
burst blood vessel in the cerebral cortex
to completely alter our perception of
reality." One of my favorite comparisons is what was said about energy.*

I watched Jill on Oprah *in an interview.
She and Oprah discussed the topic
from* MY STROKE OF INSIGHT. *Jill
commented that whoever comes into
the room has to be responsible for the*

energy they bring. I identify with this and tell my experience in my book. I kicked my own mother and my best friend of thirty-plus years out of my ICU room. My mother was so filled with fear she radiated fear of me dying. Rightfully so. My younger sister died in a hospital during childbirth. My eyesight was compromised after my brain bleed, and what I could make out of my mother's face and her energy was so awful. I had to kick her out. I did not want her fear energy and her melodramatic dreary fear, fear of me dying.

After a brain injury, your senses that are not compromised are either enhanced or diminished. My senses were all enhanced. My reality was different... So kicking my mom and my friend out seemed okay. They were the first people I saw when I woke up from my surgical procedures. I identify with this phrase "Be responsible for the energy you bring into the room." I had some odd encounters with hospital staff. I wanted them to leave.

I believe my story is told in a different form, but it is equally as powerful and educational as that of a Harvard grad-

*uate neuroscientist. The same experi-
ences are told through a gestalt collage
mixed with words and mythical beings.
It is told* IN THE COBWEBS OF MY
MIND: A Vivid and Magical Recollection of Surviving a Brain Hemorrhage.

So to all who enter, be aware of the
ENERGY *you* BRING *into the room.*

Please take responsibility for the
energy you bring into this space.

—Jill Bolte Taylor

Scene 8: Waiting for Medication and Discharge Papers / Nurses Station

Many people are in a busy place with a lot of
commotion and confusion, and suddenly Nabu and
Spider have also projected again. I begin to leave the
hospital, and Horse (My Dual Self) returns to merge
with me again. Everything shifts back to the small of
the stage, and the lights go out quickly and up when
I reach the small of the stage in front of the curtain.
This is the transition from inside the hospital to the
outside—to the bus stop.

My dual self returned like a friend and a ghost.

Scene 9: Bus Stop

The Bus Stop takes place where the opening scene took place; the curtain is shut after the lights go out. The scene takes place at the small of the stage (which I later learned was called **THE APRON**). In front of the curtain, which is now a bus stop with a bench. A proscenium stage.

I like this image. It reminds me of how I felt leaving the hospital. I wanted so much to be alone and have my independence back. I did not want to be cared for or poked with needles or questioned. This image captures the freedom and independence that I longed for. The bus stop bench waited for Nabu and Spider to show up with me so we could finish the exit scene from the hospital.

What if god was one of us, just
a stranger on the bus trying to
make his way home, what if god
was one of us, just a slob like one
of us, just a stranger on the bus
trying to make his way home.

"One of Us," a song by Joan Osborne

A paused moment at the end of the show, with the song playing. When the lights go out.

Scene 10: When the student is ready, the teacher shall appear

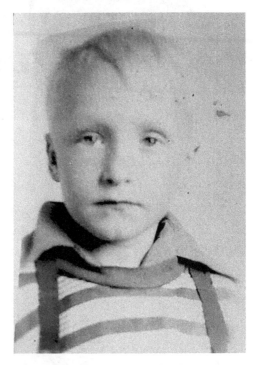

My mentor, as a young boy. He still has the same look, and I met him when he was eighty.

Set from the cafe from the opening scene back on stage. Quick set change back to the cafe. Table two chairs.

Somehow it's much later in time… clock ticking again. Maybe an actor can narrate this, or on a microphone, a voice can announce the later in time the fast forward. A man is sitting at a cafe.

My mentor, July 2022.

I walked excitedly and joined him for coffee. I am carrying a folder and a script. They are engaged in conversation. Details of conversation to be determined. Not decided on. Nabu and Spider are not determined as well, if they should be present in this scene and if the scene needs dialogue. Maybe not? Can this be a nonverbal scene left for the audience to figure out?

The End

Very End

Blast Song "Spiderweb" by Joan Osborne This song is on the same album as "One of Us." Album is titled *Relish*.

The End of Play

I added the last scene because I sensed the significance of the student/teacher friendship I was developing with my mentor. I knew it was moving me and taking me to new places artistically and creatively. It was a strong learning connection. I wanted to add it. It was through this nurturing friendship that I was able to push my dreams to new levels and believe in my story and myself even more. We would disagree on some things. But it didn't matter. It was a head spin every step of the way for me. I had to stay on my toes and keep up with the things that were flooding my mind in combination with all of Bain's opinions and ideas, suggestions, and criticism. We would argue about some things, and it could be draining and exhausting. We would have four-hour lunches… filled with intense, deep thought-provoking ideas. We covered myth and philosophy from feminism to Plato and Simone de Beauvoir.

I'm glad I was living in the world of google and spell check. I always had to look up words and theories when I got home. I was challenged by my unwillingness to see things differently and my poor listening skills. I am wildly distracted, and I have a horrible memory post-brain injury, and my concentration is selective. He is knowledgeable, precise, a good listener and serious.

This breakdown of scenes and scene transitions was one of the very first assignments from my mentor. It was designed to see if I could actually pull off how I imagined the play to run. When I still had my full script (frightening, I might add) before the downsizing. I thought I worked it out pretty well. It surprised me that it was something I thought I could do. I'm glad for my early years at the Guthrie Theater as an extra and an usher. This gave me an idea about what happened in between scenes. I sat through many rehearsals and watched numerous performances over and over again. I understood the very basics of scene changes. I could visualize it. The only trouble was the weird characters Spider, Nabu, and my dual self,

Horse. How to pull those off as actors in costumes? This was definitely a challenge. Bain helped me understand how this would be difficult, and from there, my large script was transformed into a new narrative for perhaps a one-woman show. I knew realistically that was doable.

About a year or so into our bi-monthly lunches is when they started running over four hours. The one I recall that started this trend was the day he showed up with Plato's "Allegory of the Cave." I had purchased a copy and read it, not with ease. This day was a discussion day. We had developed a pattern of going into a classroom at our lunch meetings. Later, I bought Shakespeare's *Macbeth*. It sits in a pile of books waiting to be read. It is from the No Fear Shakespeare collection. These are two pieces of literature I know I would have never bothered with if not for Bain. I plan on reading *Macbeth* after I finish this book project.

My world was really opening up.

This captures the world opening up for me, the slow, steady work of climbing that I had now been doing for years. This represents my recovery and crawling from the dark places into the light, the light of creation and storytelling.

In the beginning, I had a vision. I had to write a play. Now I was starting to see the manifestations by discovering images.

Part Two:
Structuring the Unstructured

Creativity is the power to connect
the seemingly unconnected.

—William Polomer, South
African author

Early Recovery

As I look back to tell my story, I can say that I recovered faster than most people and remained relatively intact. My small deficits, that's what they call them in the medical world, are not that noticeable on the outside. That is why they say it's an invisible injury for someone like me. Only I know the things and the struggles my brain suffered after my stroke; my brain is damaged.

There are times when I'm fully aware that my brain is not giving me what it once gave me. It's odd to reflect and be aware while stuck in the process of searching for what your brain is unable to provide at the moment! It was really bad in the beginning. I had come a long way in a year, and the two-year mark, even further. I returned to work in a restaurant after about two and a half months post-stroke, which was crazy. My neurosurgeons gave me the go. The job was both physically and mentally demanding, and restaurant people are good at multitasking. Multitasking was now in slow motion for me. I was a robot, but the robot needed a reboot; it needed to be reprogrammed. It was really frustrating not to be my old self with the uninjured brain that I knew so well. I had a new brain that I had to adjust to.

I had a manager who hired me back after the ordeal. I only worked there a couple of months before my stroke. I was fortunate to have employment with an understanding manager named Amy. When I wasn't working, I was sleeping. The fatigue that follows a brain hemorrhage is something hard to describe. I found by researching that neuro fatigue is one of the most debilitating consequences of a brain injury. Research states that it influences everything a person does, both physically and mentally. Also, it describes how it takes extra effort to do even simple tasks such as walking and talking. I remember the frustration I felt in the hospital and when I got home while recovering. I remember pushing myself really hard and overdoing everything, and wondering why I was so tired.

There was a part of me that was so out of touch with grasping what my body had just experienced. I actually thought that I was supposed to be back to normal, back to one hundred percent, the day after I was released from the hospital. I was out of touch with reality. I was not able to comprehend that my body and my brain were severely injured and that I almost died.

This physical and mental exhaustion was brought to a whole new level after my brain was injured. Depression and anxiety with post-traumatic stress are classic. So this was my new life. This type of bleeding in the brain is considered to be a Traumatic Brain Injury (TBI). I was unable to concentrate or read more than a few sentences at a time. I had headaches for a month and a half. I had blurry vision and light sensitivity, and my senses were all confused, a common side effect of brain injury. My sense of smell and taste was enhanced. I vomited easily in my first weeks of recovery. I was taking anti-seizure medication when I got home. The smell and taste of the pills I had to finish made me nauseous, because of my senses being out of whack. I had to rest my head on ice packs; they were migraine-like headaches, non-intractable tension headaches.

I had to go in for scans thinking I was going to have another rupture. I had post-traumatic stress disorder, and my anxiety was intense. My anxiety had always been bad, but now I was in fear of having another brain bleed. It's common to live in fear for a long time, my care team told me. I knew that at any given moment, something could go wrong. This was my new reality. I knew there were possibly things that could still go wrong. I had to overlook what I researched and knew. I moved forward bravely.

As time moved on, I began to get stronger. My headaches did go away. The doctor was right. I had an angiogram, an MRA, and an MRI. All my brain scans came back looking good, according to the neurosurgery and radiology team. Anticipating the results of the brain scans caused more unwanted stress. I was fully aware that it could lead to more brain surgery. I was also aware that every time they went in invasively, through the groin artery with a camera, I was at risk for a re-bleed, another stroke, coma, and/or death. Although this was rare, it was still a risk. The fear of not knowing if everything looked the way it was supposed to be was worse than living with knowing something was wrong. I dreadfully went into the hospital with great anticipation. I went to all my scheduled after-care appointments on Lorazepam. But the fear of more brain surgery or complications far outweighed the effects of the low-dose downer prescription I relied on to get myself into my appointments. It was hard to come down and settle my mind in a post-traumatic state. I was in this state for a long time. The doctors kept telling me it was normal after what I had lived through. They also assured me it would get better. It will go away, they said, and it did.

The Images

There is something about this image that captures the way the lighting looked and the feeling of September that evening my life was spared.

This image captures the feeling of biking home on the evening of my hemorrhagic stroke. I was completely fine one moment on my way home from work, the next moment in critical condition on my way to the hospital to have a life-saving intervention.

I went in search of images, and they appeared quickly and easily. It was like a scavenger hunt, and I knew exactly what I was looking for. These images were key for me to find as I began to bring my vision to life. Spiders, Nabu the Babylonian god, skulls, clocks, trees, bikes, horses, an ambulance, eyeballs, ghostly figures, hallucinations, filaments of the human brain, the brain in radiology imaging. Horse with blinders, angels, coffee shop, coils in brains and several other things. Making collages was something I did as a younger person. So looking for cool images, in general, was fun!

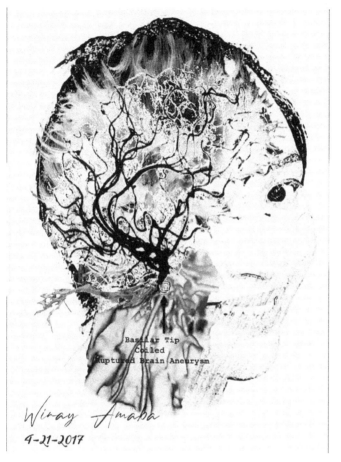

Winay Amaba Lapina, Artist.

I met Winay in an online survivor group. I like the art she created. We both suffered a hemorrhagic stroke in the same place in our brain, Basilar Tip Aneurysm. We both survived and had coils placed in our brains.

*The trees and the cobweb-like filaments in the brain
look similar to trees in radiology images.*

Big Dreams for a stage production. "I won't quit till I'm a star on Broadway." The song entered my mind as I typed big dreams for a stage production. Fun dreaming!

This bike would be a perfect prop for a play or the brochure cover. The horse and I become one, and the bike is the horse as well. It was part of the transfiguration.

*A spectacular image by Alex Andreyev, a Russian artist. It was
a surprise to learn this artist understood the same bond that
I know of. He has something written on his website about the
Nahual or Nagual, Words of Carlos Castaneda's. Another
serendipitous moment or a moment of synchronicity for me.*

A woman walking her spider as if it were her
dog. I have always made a habit of embracing the
bond between humans and animals. In the case of this
book, there was a spider that I needed to embrace.
Here is an excerpt from my first story published in
The Edge magazine. What a thrill it was. It was about
my fully realized animal spirit guide.

The Bear

It was not until I grew up and was twenty-something that I came to understand the bear's spirit and power. I learned this was my animal spirit guide that was given to me. My first totem. The bear. My Nahual.

In his book Intimate Nature, *Rigoberta Menchu tells us: "Every child is born with a nahual. The nahual is like a shadow, his protective spirit who will go through life with him. The nahual is the representative of the earth, the animal world, the sun and water, and in this way the child communicates with nature. The nahual is our double, something very important to us. Trees can be nahuals too, trees chosen by our ancestors many centuries ago."*

My full article reads like a dream. It was a series of dreams and memories of seeing the bear in my room as a child that awakened this understanding in me.

"MY MOST VIVID DREAM MEMORY FROM CHILDHOOD IS A RECURRING DREAM. BECAUSE OF MY AGE AND WHAT I WOULD LATER LEARN, I HAD NO IDEA THIS DREAM WAS SOMETHING OF GREAT IMPORTANCE AND A SACRED BLESSING."

"My dream would go like this: I would be in a dark forest with large trees that would be making noise. I was always on a path trying to reach a destination (much like Little Red Riding Hood), and then I would realize someone was following me. I would then see the bear, a very large bear, and I would be frightened. I would always try to get ahead of her by running as fast as I could, but I could never move. I was always in a paralyzed dream state.

Out of fear, I would wake up.

The oddest thing for me to grasp at such a young age was this: I grew up in a city in a large, old house, and my bedroom was on the second

*floor. I would try to fall asleep when
I'd see this huge bear's head looking
at me through my screen window.*

It was alive and very real.

*I knew in my mind that this could not
possibly be a bear. In the city? Suspend-
ed in the air, staring at me intensely?
I would see the bear's head on top of
my radiator. The bear would always
appear in a different place in my room.*

*It was not until I grew up and was
twenty-something that I came to understand the bear's spirit and power.
I learned this was my animal spirit guide that was given to me. My
first totem. The bear. The Nahual.*

In his book,, Intimate Nature, *Rigoberta Menchu tells us, "Every child is
born with a nahual. The nahual is like
a shadow, his protective spirit who will
go through life with him. The nahual
is the representative of the earth, the
animal world, the sun, and water, and
in this way, the child communicates
with nature. The nahual is our double,
something very important to us. Trees
can be nahuals too, trees chosen by*

our ancestors many centuries ago."

*I used to struggle with rage and anger.
I had an explosive temper, and I would
fight—especially when justice was
deserved. I often think there is an angry,
wild bear that lives and expresses itself
deep from within me. My calm side is
the bear in hibernation, and the awake
bear is the part of me that most people regret to know. Including myself.*

*Now that I'm older, the bear befriended
me in a new way. She rears and stands
tall to support me and continues to
guide me. I had a beautiful dream about
her last summer. It took place at Hidden
Beach, on the east side of Cedar Lake in
Minneapolis. The dream went like this...*

*People were running in panic around
in the woods behind the beach, saying,
"Oh my, have you seen the bear?" They
were frightened because there are no
bears in the city. I had to walk through
the woods to see the bear. She was on
her hind legs standing in the sand by
the shoreline—and she was mine. She
came back to me after all these years.
She appeared very much like a pet to me
in this dream. Others were in awe that I*

was not frightened of her. She was glow-
ing in the sun and appeared as if she
was being worshipped, by me anyway.

The message was clear. When I
awoke the next morning, I was so
thankful and happy to have recon-
nected with my childhood guide.
She surprises me when I least expect
it. I'm humbled and grateful."

My counterparts are always available for me to shapeshift into. And as I've aged, I've managed to pick up a few more along the way. They have appeared at different times in my life. They come on strong and are undeniable. They come with a mission in mind. They are **REAL**.

*I waited for the ambulance here, at the coffee shop.
I somehow became aware of my mortality both
my dual and me. The clock was ticking, time was
crucial. Or death was surely coming soon.*

Time

Horse skulls

Human Skull

The images of both a horse and a human skull plus the clock, I strongly connected with. I knew my time was limited and death was near unless I got to the hospital fast. My survival instincts took over. The clock was ticking. I somehow knew this during my brain hemorrhage. Although I had no idea what was happening in my moment of crisis.

I found images that portrayed what I wanted for my play! I thought these would be backdrops with the sound of a clock ticking for the opening scene of my play!

Time

Plus horse and bike equal life in my case.

Brain Injury Radio

I spent two years studying all the medical facts about my brain injury. I had networked with many other survivors. I was even a guest on *Brain Injury Radio* (talk radio) and was going to host a show.

I hosted one show and considered doing it permanently, but it was not for me. I am a writer. I wanted to write about it.

I had researched a lot. I had my medical records. I learned a lot and met people in online groups and discovered their stories in their blogs. Some of the people I met on the internet were not so lucky. Some were in wheelchairs and with walkers for life. Some were blind in one eye or both. Some lived with debilitating headaches every day. My bad headaches only lasted about six weeks. Another person was dragging a limb, and some were in medically induced comas for six months and had to learn to walk and talk again. So many beautiful people have an entire side of their face drooping. They always had the before and after comparison photos. Some had part of their skull replaced with plastic. Some with dents in their heads and foreheads. The horror of craniotomy scars and staples all over the head in every direction. This was a bad monster movie with swollen faces and bruised eyes, and staples all over the shaved bald head. I was and remain lucky. I was always reminded of all the things that could have happened to me. That didn't.

Here I stand still intact. My brain was damaged in a place that created a visual field cut. A minor visual deficit. I call it my trick eye. It flares up on bad days and under stress, but some days I do not notice it. I have memory issues, and sometimes too much stimulation is overload, which is very common statistically for brain injury survivors. It is called sensory overload. Something I'm very well acquainted with. My brain has compensated and re-taught itself. It's adjusted to seeing a new way. It was horrible in the early part of recovery. My short-term memory is way worse. There is much evidence that supports that if you live through this, you will have anxiety and memory issues for the rest of your life. It was the consensus among my fellow survivors. All health professionals know it. They all told me it's common. I'm on a very low dose of a miracle drug for anxiety that is used to treat multiple things. Many people take 100 milligrams or more. I take 30 milligrams, sometimes 20. *Amitriptyline generic name for Elavil: treats pain and depression and helps with sleep and neuropathic, nerve pain, and head pain. It came out in the 1960s.* I have pain in my skull and nerve damage where they drilled a hole in my head to place the tube into a ventricle in my brain. There was a sore spot. It was always sensitive, and it itched most of the time. It finally got better after two and a half years. It still flares up. My neck has never felt the same, and I doubt it ever will.

Medical Research

The research started in my recovery right away as soon as I could concentrate enough and read more than a few sentences. With a visual field cut, it took a while for my brain to rearrange and compensate. I realized I was spared. I did not have any of the complications that can follow and kill you. This intrigued me to study all this information. I became obsessed with medical research. Just ask any of my family or close friends. They would receive random texts or emails from medical journals of information on a medical fact. Sometimes I would send them the monster horror photos of other survivors that had it so much worse than I did.

At some point, I requested my medical records from the hospital. It's strange to read about Jane Doe when she is you. I remember reading a doctor's notes in my medical records who had been observing me. He said they were monitoring me closely, and I was at risk for sudden and fatal neurological deterioration. I researched so much before I wrote the play. I studied endovascular coiling and aneurysm repair. I had the coiling procedure. I studied the placement of the tube into the ventricle of my brain (ventriculostomy). The first script or drafts I wrote of my play were loaded with medical information.

There are major complications that can occur just hours or days after your life is initially saved. I was in the ICU for two weeks and managed to avoid dying from some of the complications I discovered later in my research, the grim reality that I escaped.

The following are medical complications after suffering a subarachnoid hemorrhage.[4]

Vasospasm: This occurs when an artery narrows due to a persistent contraction. "A spasm" of the blood vessel. This narrowing can reduce blood flow to parts of the brain. My medical records state I had a couple of small ones.

Hydrocephalus: A blood clot can lodge and prevent drainage. I had a tube in the ventricle of my brain to prevent this. The cerebrospinal fluid (CSF) would have nowhere to go. It would put pressure on the brain and skull. I was monitored for the

4   www.verywellhealth.com

pressure in my skull until the tube was removed. Intracranial pressure can lead to coma and decreased consciousness. This can result in death.

Seizures: Blood can irritate the cerebral cortex and result in a seizure. A small number of people go on to develop epilepsy. Doctors may consider using preventative anti-epileptic medication. I was on them during my stay in the hospital and was sent home with them. I took them for a few weeks and was instructed to make sure to take them all. I was lucky. I was spared from seizures in my recovery and to this day.

Rebleeding After Subarachnoid Hemorrhage: Patients are at risk for rebleeding within the first twenty-four hours. To prevent this, the aneurysms are sealed off by clipping or coiling. I had the coiling procedure done through a catheter in the groin artery.

While these four main complications seem like enough things that can go wrong, unfortunately, there are several others. Deep vein thrombosis of the legs for one and many others.

I managed to survive, and when I recovered enough, I read my medical records. I felt I was reading about someone else. It was surreal.

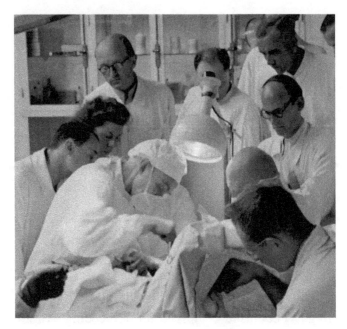

This surgery was performed on me. A ventriculostomy
and the coiling of the ruptured aneurysm.

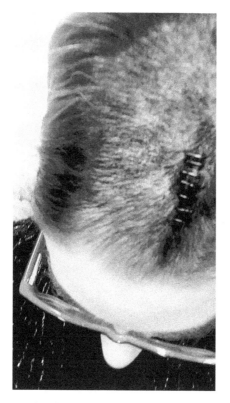

The day my staples were removed.

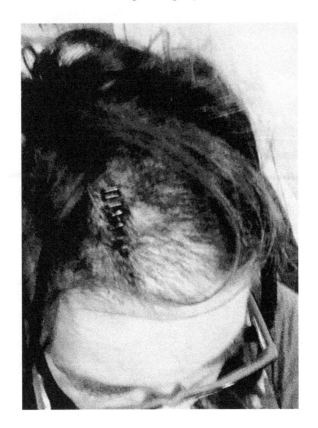

Horse / Nabu / Spider

The imagery of a derby horse with blinders, in my original story, is symbolic of seeing straight ahead. Tunnel vision it was, and I had it. I knew, without question, I had to get to the hospital, and I did. My survival instincts took over in such a way that I immediately knew I would die if I did not get to a hospital. I hate going to any doctor. I suffer from white coat syndrome: A condition where a patient's blood pressure is higher when taken in a clinical or medical setting than it is in other settings. I get panicky and anxious just walking into a hospital or clinical setting. The horse was the part of me that saved my life.

Photo by Jeanne Günesoglu.

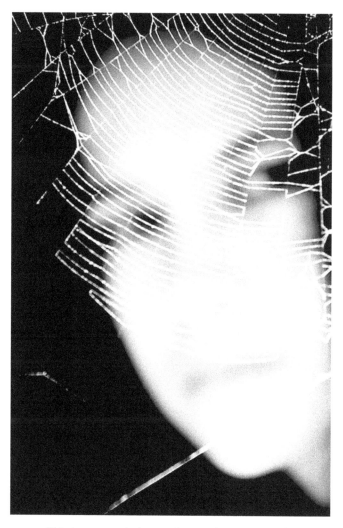

This image reminds me of me and my story in the
cosmic space, in the cobwebs of my mind.

Self Portrait.

I took my time with this project, writing and exploring. As I explored in depth, the web became clearer. The magic was real. Living in the world of my memory and living inside the web was an alternate reality. Both were real for me as I wove my gestalt story. I wove it as my dual self and my other self. Not sure who was more important. Which voice was dominant?

As I write my story I would write through the eyes and minds of Spider and Nabu as well. I merged with my characters as if I had multiple personalities. I had to think like them and act like them.

The sketches I did of my dual self came after I tried too hard to sketch a perfect horse. My mentor guided and directed me into an exercise. He said when you sketch, sketch as if you were in the hospital in your bed during the moment of crisis, and the only way you could communicate was with a chalkboard in hand and a white drawing stick. This drawing above came first, and the others followed.

My first sketches were tight and contrived without freedom. These are loose.

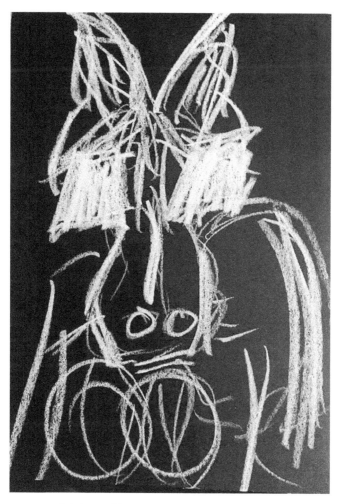

*My horse blinders. I titled this **My Picasso**.*

Megan Bacigalupo

Nora Truelson, Artist.

The horse lends himself to me to shapeshift into. I detach myself from my body to escape the pain of my brain bleeding. My dual took over. At this point, I was already starting to die, but this horse with blinders, running in the derby to the finish line, aka the hospital, is what saved me. I had become familiar with the act of shapeshifting at a young age around the time I started learning about horses and riding. It was escapism, a fantasy, a mechanism. Transfiguration was magic, and I learned the craft of it as a young person when I was in the fourth and fifth grades. I used to pretend I was a horse when I was young. I used to set up a hunter-jumper course in the backyard. The top half of me was the rider, the bottom half of me the horse. I used to pretend I was showing. I would jump over tipped-over picnic benches and odd improvised cavaletti. I wrote a story about it. I titled it "Shapeshifting." This, too, is in my collection of writing in *The Edge* magazine. This story came out in 2015.[5]

> *It was the Bell witch and the spir-*
> *its from Cave Rock at Lake Tahoe*
> *that came to me when I asked*
> *the spirit guides for help.*
>
> *It was all the animals and the magical*
> *people that got me shape-shifting again.*
>
> *The owl got my attention, along*
> *with many spiders and moths.*

---

5   https://www.edgemagazine.net/2015/05/shape-shift-ing/

Mick Jagger's magical pow-
er inspired me, as well.

Saint Joan of Arc.

The sharks and dolphins being
taken from the waters, the tol-
erance for war and evil,

That the creatures cry out about.
The music of fall, "No Sym-
pathy for the Devil"

No Sympathy for the Devil

I remember becoming half horse as a child. I
had a really good friend whose dad had a beautiful
horse ranch in Red Wing, Minnesota. I went down
there on weekends, and I learned a lot about
horses. I learned to ride on a Shetland pony named
Ginger.

When I got back to the city, I set up a hunter
jumper course in my family's backyard and pretended
that the bottom of my body was a horse that would
be walking, trotting, cantering, galloping part of me,
and the top of me was the person or the rider. I felt
one with the horse. I would make horse sounds, and
then, as the child, being the rider, I instructed the
horse and gave commands. I was in second, third,
and fourth grade when I did this.

Much later in life, while discovering ancient art and myth, I was thrilled to find among Egyptian art half-beast and half-human figures. I really understood this.

People have always been one with animals.

As I grew into my teens, I realized that I could eventually take on the energy of any living animal, transfigure in fantasy and spirit, receive the energy of the animal, and understand its power, and be it. I got into the animal rights movement, but it was so painful that I had to stop bombarding myself with facts and images. It hurt me as if I was the animal upon which cruelty was inflicted. To this day, if I see images of animal abuse, I'm ill for days, sometimes weeks.

In many ways, I'm always in turmoil, and I care, yet I'm helpless on all levels. Facing it is a harsh reality. In 2007, when I became educated and aware of the slaughtering of the dolphins in Japan, I was in my fully awakened Kundalini state, and I became ill. I felt victimized, and I still do. I was horrified at what greed and evil were doing to this mammal, to the apes in Africa, and to pigs and chickens kept in concentration camps across this nation.

When I heard of the dolphin issues, everything I had accumulated throughout my life resurfaced. My passion for animals seemed to haunt me, and I realized I was unable to escape this part of myself; as much as I would like to block it out, I cannot. I am ill to this day over all of it.

I had the most profound experience. I was napping and was out of my body. In astral travel. I saw a huge eye of a dolphin who was being killed. I heard her cry in pain. She cried, blood ran down her body and she thanked me and told me in spirit that she was glad I cared and that other people cared. It was bittersweet that a dolphin acknowledged me.

I do not live in Japan and nowhere near the ocean. The dolphin and I were one.

> "I said to my soul, be still, and let
> the dark come upon you which
> shall be the darkness of God."

—T. S. Eliot

There was something powerful about remembering this when I began to connect to the horse as an adult. The horse is again at the end of the story. The horse brings the story full circle. When my traveling companions show up to greet me, Spider and Nabu, the horse makes a big statement as he walks down the hospital halls making a huge splash with the sound of hooves clipping… Spider and Nabu are quiet. The horse steals the show right before the end. Then kindly allows the spider and Nabu to finish it. Spider and Nabu walk out with me and sit quietly at the bus stop with me. I saw the horse one last time. I double-take him. He is gone. I am accompanied by my writer's totem Spider and god of wisdom and writing. At the bus stop, I again take one final look to make sure he is gone… He is gone. He did his job.

Spider and Nabu: Backstory

I got really into spiders many years ago, not by choice. It was long before my subarachnoid brain hemorrhage. I was mysteriously getting spider bites. I found it highly unusual. I live in the city, in an apartment building. I have spent many summers of my life in northern Minnesota, in the woods, without ever getting a single bite. I am allergic to pretty much everything. I have always had bad reactions to any kind of bug or insect bites. I got a scary, bad reaction to the spider's bite, the venom. I was searching bites on www.BadSpiderBites.com. My bites looked like all of the bad bites. I narrowed it down to the types of spiders. I killed a couple in my apartment. I bought all kinds of repellent, natural and poisonous. These bites were recurring yearly bites. They only occurred from June through August. I would get three or four a year. The spiders had me researching their venom and how everybody processes the venom differently. My bites disturbed me enough to consider it something more than a bite. That is when I discovered that the spider is the writer's totem. I also discovered and considered the possibility of it being a curse that was put on me by a practitioner of dark magic, a witch. In my studies of magic over the years, I knew this was a possibility. A spell (curse) that needed to be broken. On the other hand, it could have been a cycle in nature. I went with a cycle of nature theory. Nonetheless, the spider hugely got my attention. My allergic reaction to the venom, which ran an ugly course, could hardly be denied. I still somewhat question my sanity with this whole spider bite experience. This was a yearly episodic occurrence that recurred for several years. My magical thinking couldn't resist this. The story that Spider and Nabu were originally in was about Mick Jagger. He was a modern-day pantheon god. He was some sort of spirit guide or twin soul. In this story, the spider bite put me into a coma. This story also is where Nabu came to me as the god of writing. I dropped the story. I had writer's block.

A sketch I did years ago of Mick Jagger. It hangs
in my kitchen next to an image of Frida Kahlo
and my sister Andrea, who is deceased.

After my brain hemorrhage, I revisited it. I was
completely floored that these characters also were so
easy and ready to join my new story. I will never

forget the thrill when the lightbulb lit up spider in the subarachnoid space in my brain, working in sync with this god, Nabu. They had taken a long nap in my dusty notes and in my laptop with all the other data. They were wanting and had waited to be born properly. This was their intended place. I had goosebumps. They found their home. I found new inspiration. So this is how they became my muses. My ah-ha moment! I went into a coma in my Mick Jagger story. This was a frightening prophetic realization. In this coma, Nabu throws letters at me. They hang in the cobwebs, which later in the story become the filaments of my brain. I was already on this path, pre-hemorrhage. They told me telepathically (in the original story) that I needed to record my story. If I recorded it, I would then be released from the coma, the web. This was three years before my near-death incident, my life-changing hemorrhagic stroke. I have always been into Native American spirituality, animal totems, and the like. None of this was unusual to me. The Bear was my first animal guide which started in my childhood years.

I had lots of prints of spiders, and I sketched some. I discovered exotic spiders. They look like tribal warriors and tribal priests and priestesses. These spiders have undeniable power and mystery.

The Horse, Nabu, and Spider were the glue in my original script. They wove the story together and provided a beginning, middle, and end. I desperately needed this, especially having not a clue about how to write a play. So they became my friends as I brought them to life. Even more so as I sketched them and decided how they might look in the images and the sketches.

My Finished sketch of Nabu, the Babylonian
god of wisdom and writing, a scribe.

Nabu – A Scribe.

Sculpted bronze figure by Lee Lawrie. Door

detail, east entrance, Library of Congress.

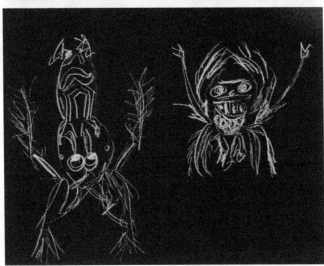

I sketched these as I discovered peacock spiders, they reminded me of tribal warriors, priests, and priestesses.

Exotic spiders are extraordinary.

Putting it all together

Into the cosmos I went. I was here all along. I found myself deep into comparisons, into astrophysics and theories studied by Nasa research physicists. I had entered the web-like filaments of my brain. I was inside the CAT scan and the MRI. I was traveling through my arteries in the catheter of the angiogram. Scientists have now stated in theory that the human brain and the cosmic web are remarkably similar. Everything we know came from cosmic explosions billions of years ago. I also discovered in my research that we are in a constant state of decay and regeneration, according to scientists. I became fascinated with the cobwebs in my own mind (brain) and fascinated that there was a subarachnoid and an arachnoid space in my brain that conveniently awaited a spider. I discovered and developed a

141

character for my play. I had found a rhythm and a beat in the cosmos, a reflection that shone on my play from the dark, murky spaces of the black holes and vast darkness of the cosmos. It was in this darkness that the sketches on the black paper came to life and became my inspiration for my book, the one-woman show, and documentary film. I tried to create them all in my mind… in my injured brain.

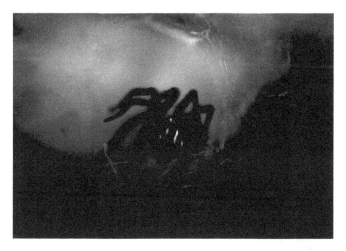

Amazing comparisons of the universe and a spider's web.

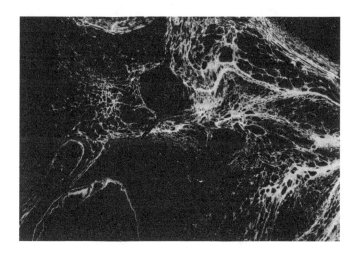

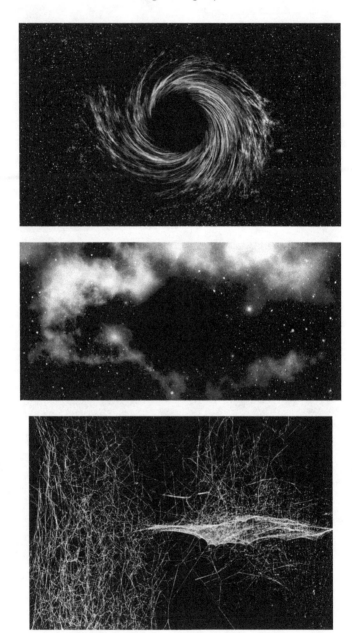

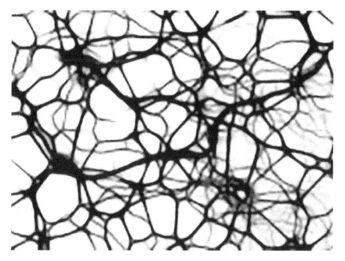

When I began writing my play, I stumbled upon a book in a Little Free Library titled *Big Magic: Creative Living Beyond Fear* by Elizabeth Gilbert. The cover reads *#1 New York Times Bestselling Author of* Eat Pray Love. I was facing my dreams and fears at the same time, and with determination, discipline, and drive, I kept pressing on as my play changed from a script to a different narrative. I dove deep into the cosmos. I had a ritual of listening to the same music every time I wrote and edited. I later wrote the narrative and sketched and cut out and pasted images or worked in the box (the assignment from my mentor). While developing my project and working on the creative elements I listened to the music of Neil Young, Joan Baez, Simon and Garfunkel, Bob Dylan, James Taylor, Kate Wolf, Joni Mitchell, and an occasional "Puff the Magic Dragon" would sound. I alternated between these stations on my Pandora radio station on my iPhone. There is something about listening to the oldies, these types of artists that were in their heyday in the 60s and 70s. There is something inspirational about imagining them all on the rise in New York City back in the day. You can almost picture the Chelsea Hotel and the clubs, the hangouts in the village. You almost wish or imagine going back in time and pretending you might just be getting started with your craft with all of them. Drinking and chain smoking cigarettes. I can see the smoke-filled rooms vividly. The music was inspiring and kept me on task, as it became a ritual.

I guess it is safe to say it looks like the stars did line up for me when I met my mentor. He directed and guided my creativity and helped enhance my mind and writing. He taught me new ways of looking at things, challenged me intellectually, and forced me into philosophical thinking. Every time we got together or had an email exchange, I would quickly find myself looking up definitions of words, books or artists. It was hard at first to keep up with his creativity and knowledge. As I got to know him, it never became any easier. To this day, it's always a pop quiz at lunch, and he reminds me of how little I know. Sometimes I like to remind myself that he was in army intelligence in Berlin when the wall went up before I was born. He is humble and kind, yet he can reduce and interrogate me in a way I've never experienced. I think it is part of his teaching style. Our first meetings reminded me of college classes, the kind that gave you a headache because you had to learn to use your brain in new ways. The classes were philosophy, math, logic, science, religion, theology, mythology, art, sketching, and metaphysics combined. He spoke in higher realms yet remained humbled. I tried to keep up with him. I remember when he suggested I start sketching on black paper with a white drawing stick. I found this to be a struggle. I asked him if I could switch from black paper to white paper and use a black charcoal drawing stick. It seemed more natural to me. As a younger person, I took a few art classes using charcoal. He said no, and in one of our email exchanges, he said, "I think the black void is important for theatrical reasons... painting fine art happens on white canvas, theater on a black and silent one...theater shines a light into the darkness and breaks the silence with sound." I remember this really stood out to me, and suddenly I was able to visualize this whole thing in black and white, and then as I sketched, the beautiful song by Simon and Garfunkel, "The Sound of Silence," came on.

Next are the actual events of the catastrophic day. A day I will never forget, September 20, 2017. I added some lines that were written for my original script titled "Subarachnoid." This was before it evolved into the possibility of a one-woman show or a documentary film. Originally, I planned to have a narrator or actor recite a line from my medical records. Then finish the scene with medical facts about the scene. I thought this would create a smooth consistency or rhythm to wrap up the scene changes. I envisioned this. It was also a medical fact and statistics play, but my creativity got the best of me. Yet, I did not exclude this entirely. It is in this next segment that I bring these facts to life. It became a dancing, moving project. I share the images, the images that helped me create my vision. I share the drawings that my mentor guided me into. He brought the world of sketching by provoking my thoughts and moving me into the crisis, into the immediacy of the moment. I was reliving my crisis but as the character in my play, as if I were another person on top of my dual self. The actor was another self I imagined. As I began to sketch in the moment of the crisis, I became an actor with a chalkboard and a white drawing stick as a character (my character) in my hospital bed. I sketched the mythical figures and my dual self, the horse. I write descriptively, adding the sound effects by writing the words of the sounds for the reader to imagine. I imagined them for my play.

Part Three
Merging Two Tracks

It is during our darkest moments
that we must focus to see the light.

—Aristotle

September 20, 2017:
The Night I Lived

It was a warm September evening in 2017. I unlocked a city bike out of the bike docks, which were a couple of blocks away from my uptown Minneapolis restaurant job. Not too far from home. I remember coasting slowly toward home, enjoying the beautiful weather. I remember the pants I was wearing and the light autumn scarf. I remember the shoulder bag I was carrying. I can feel the air temperature and how the early night sky appeared. Looking back, I had an odd or unusual sense of clarity. I was so familiar with the route home. I could have easily ridden home blindfolded. I always passed a friend's apartment. If his lights were on, I would often hoot like an owl when I passed by his window. He would always tell me later that he saw me or heard me. As I continued down the quiet city street, there was an inner silence and peace that swept over me. I felt alert and content. A heavy stillness came over me. The moment seemed crisp and is still sharp in my memory. The large trees from both sides of the street created an arch over me like a blanket that covered me. Looking back on this night, it appears to me as a scene in a movie. I can envision myself as an actress, or I can see an actress playing my part. I become my character as I write this.

There are combinations of lines I wrote and excerpts from my original essay and my actual medical records and medical facts from research.

My body became a clock, time pushed forward as a force. I felt like a derby horse with blinders, all I could see was the ambulance that I imagined.

(Tick tick tick, clock ticking loud, sirens loud, flashing light red light, the ambulance and sounds of street traffic.)

I heard a whooshing sound in my ears. I was going partially deaf, and my vision was getting shaky and blurred. The pain in my head was hard for my body to contain. It clamped so hard, gripping my entire head and neck as if a sledgehammer had hit hard. A thunderclap headache. *I shape-shifted into the horse.*

I could not possibly endure this pain any longer. I was outside my body and completely detached. I turned off the side street and headed to the nearest public place for help. The Spyhouse coffee shop in my neighborhood.

I handed the city bike off and told this guy on his cell phone to call me an ambulance. I instinctively knew something was very wrong. A woman helped me sit at an outdoor cafe table and gave me a cool cloth. As I waited for the ambulance, I was able to process that something so foreign was happening to my entire body. I was in shock. I was already miles away, outside my body. There is no real way to describe this pain to someone who has not experienced it. It grips your entire being. I gave up control. In the moment of surrender, a surge of calm came over me. I was in new territory and surprisingly still in my mind and body. A state of serenity swept over me as if I was somewhat content. I still knew the clock was ticking. Time was something I knew was key to survival.

All of this was happening so fast, and I was able to process it knowing what I needed to do. Without a doubt, I knew I needed to get to the hospital. It was built-in awareness. I knew I needed rescuing. I remember hearing the sirens. I knew they were for me. I recall the feeling of not knowing, and it's hard to describe the unknowingness and the vulnerability which became me. When the paramedics arrived, I was surprisingly and interestingly conscious and alert. I was conscious long enough to get the words of my symptoms out of my mouth. I remember the helplessness that I melted into. I found it interesting that I was calm and not panicked. The independent and self-reliant me had just shifted into the dependent and reliant self. I lost my independence. The surrender became real here. I still was aware of the time. My survival instincts knew what they were doing.

In the ambulance, I vomited twice. I remember looking into the paramedic's eyes. I'll never forget his eyes. He was all I had to hold onto; our eyes were locked. I had to trust him, a total stranger. I managed to stay conscious all the way downtown, and he even asked me what hospital I wanted to go to. I said Hennepin County Medical Center. I had a favorite and brilliant doctor at this hospital, Dr. Scott Davies. He was modest and well-liked by his patients and colleagues. He was regularly written up in the Twin Cities and America's top doctors in magazines. The paramedic gave me something for nausea and helped me lay down on the stretcher gurney. I was slowly fading. He and his partner pushed me into the ER, and it was there that I started to drift. I knew that I was going. I wasn't sure where I was drifting to. It was peaceful, without pain. Fading, I was fading out. I was not resisting. I knew I had no control over what my body was doing.

This was my last memory of pre-surgery. I remember bouncing on the gurney as they wheeled me out of the ambulance. I heard the sounds of the ER's busy entrance. I remember passing by the desk, and people were looking at me.

My medical records state that I arrived unresponsive and moaning. I was told later, and I read in my medical records that I was going blind… that I was hysterical and yelling… I'm going blind. I also learned that some of the staff were unsure if I was a psychiatric patient. I have no memory of these last few details.

> *The subarachnoid space is where the cerebrospinal fluid circulates and is responsible for protecting your brain from injury. Serving as a cushion. A hemorrhage in this space can cause a coma, paralysis and even death.*
> —Healthline.com

The following images are a depiction of me arriving at the hospital. Disconnecting from my dual self.

In the Cobwebs of My Mind

Lots of information was provided in my medical records, including conversations I had with people who worked in the hospital and remembered me when I returned for aftercare. I learned that I was scanned and prepped for surgery. I had suffered a hemorrhagic stroke and a brain bleed in the subarachnoid space in my brain. Lights out for me until I woke up in the ICU the next day.

Lines:

Megan: I'm going blind, I can't see. Take me to Hennepin County Medical Center. I have to vomit. My neck, my head.

Medical Records/Doctor: I affirm that this patient is critically ill and is at risk for sudden and fatal neurological deterioration due to subarachnoid hemorrhage.

Fact Research: Subarachnoid space refers to the space where cerebrospinal fluid circulates and is responsible for protecting your brain, serving as a cushion. A hemorrhage in this space can cause coma, paralysis, and even death.

As the drugs kicked in and flooded my veins,
A drill pierced my skull to create a hole for the fluid

to drain, and a tube was inserted into the ventricle of my brain. The coils were also secured in my brain; they were inserted through the femoral artery in my groin. The doctors placed titanium coils in my brain to fix the ruptured aneurysm.

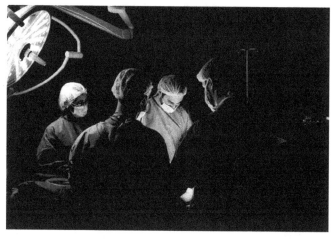

Suddenly they made their entrance. Nabu, the Babylonian god of wisdom and writing was accompanied by a spider. This spider occupied the subarachnoid space in my brain. They spoke to me in a kind of synchronicity, telepathically. Nabu said, "I hold the destiny of people. I have the power to shorten or add years to your life. I am the god of wisdom and writing. I am associated with Wednesday, and today is Wednesday. I will help you move between worlds. I, too, dwell inside your brain with a spider." He then said to me, "Spider is the writer's totem. We are here to teach you about death and rebirth. Don't ignore us..." Nabu then tossed letters and numbers into my subarachnoid space. Spider used all eight of her legs and spread many alphabets in different directions and languages... some were primordial, some pictographs. Spider then said, "Nabu is the keeper of these letters. I am associated with magic. In the web so are you. We exist in the cobwebs of your mind. This is your reality." Nabu told me he held the cards, and he was holding me. As he disappeared, he threw more letters at me like in the game of Scrabble.

I could see them hanging in the filaments of the trabecular connective tissues of my brain. I saw Spider hanging in there, too. She was helping me sort all the letters and alphabets. The letters mixed with my blood and cerebrospinal fluid. The fluid was draining out of the top of my head through a tube. There was a whirlpool of letters, blood, and cerebrospinal fluid. The letters were trying to exit, but thanks to Spider, they stayed. With her eight legs, she caught them in the suction of the drain.

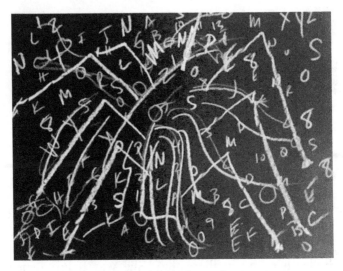

An early sketch I did. My brain during surgery.

This is how I imagined the scene in the one-woman show. My mentor had a flash of something in a conversation. We discussed rolling backdrops with images for the one-woman show. This would be in the surgery scene as a backdrop for part of the scene. The other image that came to me was a spider's web, also the radiology of the brain. I see this backdrop with the huge square letters in the game of scrabble with Spider in there somewhere as well what I describe as scrabble letters and numbers inside my brain with Spider. Accompanied by the sound of the drill as it penetrated my skull and a layer of my brain. I picture this with lights and sounds. The sound of the drill going into the skull matter. The lights flash. I see this in black and white.

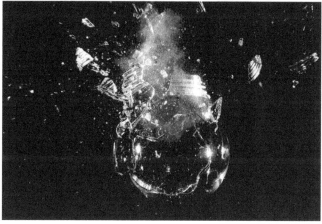

These images capture my attention. It depicts the shattering of my skull as the drill burrows its way into my skull and a layer of my brain.

Sound of the drill, drilling into the skull. Strobe lights flash with an image like this above and alternate between the alphabet.

Lines: *We are here to teach you. We exist in the cobwebs of your mind. Keeper of letters associated with magic. This is your reality. In the web of your brain. These primordial alphabets hold power.*

Medical Record: *Drill type/twist right frontal lobe, intervention complete/ successful/ coils placed in brain. Ventric drain placed.*

Fact: *In the human brain, cerebrospinal fluid is located in the subarachnoid space between the arachnoid and the pia mater.*

Post-Surgery Company

I was intubated, and the drugs were wearing off. I was now breathing on my own but had no idea when I started to. I was later informed. Through extremely blurry vision, I came into full consciousness and saw my mother and my close friend Nora. They were standing around my bed. Even on hardcore pain medication, my throat was so sore. I was in pain. It was from being intubated. My vision was awful, and even after my glasses were placed back on, it was still terrible. I could barely see. I remember pointing at my mother's eye and saying, "I can't see your eye." I had suffered a field of vision cut. My stroke caused brain damage in that part of my brain. The one thing I could make out was my mother's face and how she looked. It was a look of intense fear, almost as if she was paralyzed in fear. My younger sister had died about thirteen years before this medical crisis. She died in a hospital.

I'm sure my mother thought she was now going to have another daughter die. Her face looked like I was going to die. I could not bear to look at her. I asked about my cat. My friend Nora assured me my apartment neighbor-friend (Colleen) was caring for her. I was attached to a pole with a tube in my brain. I was hooked on all sorts of things and drugged. This pole was now an extension of my body and my brain. It was unsettling, and it bothered me. They started getting me up, and this time I walked. I was not crippled, and I could talk. These were milestones at beating the odds of suffering a hemorrhagic stroke. Everything was wrong. I was confused and agitated. The heat was too hot and then too cold. The food guy kept bringing me meatballs, and I am vegetarian. It was too loud, then too quiet. I was becoming a pain-in-the-ass patient. I was a bitch to everyone, including the smiling guy cleaning the bathroom. The idiot who kept bringing me meatballs. I told them every day I was vegetarian. The annoying people were assessing me, trying to psychoanalyze me. Which I later refused. A social worker who thought I gave a shit about whatever they were prematurely trying to assess. This was bullshit, and I was going crazy. All I wanted was more pain meds and to sleep. Impossible sleep.

Lines: *Do you know what day*
it is? Do you know your name?
Do you know where you are?

Lines: *I can't see! My cat, my cat?*
Who is taking care of her?

Doctor/Nurse: *Interestingly patient*
noticed a visual field cut when she
came into the ER; she continues to
have a visual field cut. She is under
very close neurological observation.
Being monitored. She appears relatively
intact. The patient currently menstru-
ating, and her behavior is calm with
intermittent anxious behavior noted.
With new tasks or multiple tasks.

Fact: *A hemorrhagic stroke is a*
life-threatening condition with a high
mortality rate. Many deaths occur
within the first two days. Many die
before even reaching the hospital.

One of my lifelong friends (Dan) biked all the way downtown to see me in the hospital. I was not in the mood for company, and I told him. He was not pleased and ignored my request to leave. "I just biked all the way here and you're asking me to leave?" he said. There was a nurse in the room with us. There was a constant flow of nurses: 1st, 2nd, and 3rd shifts. They all talked to me upon arrival and reviewed the summary notes from the previous shifts, and they always had a comment about something that happened on the last shift. I was sure not one of them liked me. I was told when I got home how completely awful my behavior was. I was hell on wheels. I'm sure of it. My family and friends did a great job of refreshing my failed memory due to my traumatic brain injury. They enjoyed telling me how awful I was in the ICU. My mom even cracked a joke saying the nurses were drawing straws when it came to who had to take care of you. Dan sat with me, and I got my spaghetti without the meatball and the yogurt with coffee.

I eventually woke up after a rest and noticed my chest was itching. There was a port attached with adhesive. I was developing an allergic reaction to the sticky glue. I wanted to remove it. But the nurse said no. She brought me anti-itch cream. I was extremely irritated. *I was observed as anxious, afraid, apprehensive, and frustrated. I stated that I felt hopeless and was angry.*

Nothing in the medical world could relieve me of my miserable existence. My mental and emotional state was not well. The staff was arranging for a psychologist and a physical therapist to pay me a visit. Why the fuck would I want to see either of them. I had a tube coming out of my fucking brain, and my blood mixed with my cerebrospinal fluid and drained into a bag. I was focused on that alone. I could not walk anywhere but to the bathroom with my pole with my brain drain and with the help of people. I was in a bad mood. I got my period in the ICU. I had blood coming out of both ends. A nurse told me all women get their periods in the ICU. It is brought on by trauma.

I refused to cooperate with any kind of formal assessment. The staff from social services or psyc staff gave me dirty looks. I did not like their attitudes. I hated the way that this type of doctor or service thinks they can help you. When really they haven't lived a minute in your crisis (shoes) and have no clue what you're dealing with. I remember one woman's presence (energy) bothered me so much. I wanted her out of the room. I did not want anyone around me. They assume there is a formula to follow, and like magic, if you do as they say, things will get better. They forget to take many things into account. Like I was up for counseling (haha), what a joke; they ask idiotic questions and stare at you in a condescending, pathetic way. Who has time for that shit when they have a tube coming out of a ventricle of their brain and are higher than a kite on meds and hallucinating from interrupted sleep? NOT ME. Someone placed a tub of warm water with special soap and a washcloth for a sink bath. I was too busy talking on the phone and watching TV. When you watch television after a brain injury, you have no idea what is going on. It was a background distraction. I refused to have a sink bath.

I was in a teaching hospital. There was a team of doctors all at various levels in their medical training. About six or seven of them stood at the foot of my bed staring at me with straight faces like I was an alien or miracle or both. One wore a turban and had a beard. Lots of neurosurgeons are from India. The lead doctor was of Indian descent but was most likely born here and had no accent. He did all the talking and was in charge. He was pleasant and told me how lucky I was and how good I looked. He did some tests on me to measure my strength and see how well I could follow his finger with my eyes.

I told him about my headaches, and he told me about how the brain hates blood and, unfortunately, the headaches have a way of sticking around. He explained the dangers of post-surgical complications and explained them. He assured me they were carefully monitoring these in my case. He confirmed the results of the MRI that was ordered earlier.

Lines: *The brain hates blood. Squeeze my fingers, follow my fingers with your eyes, and look at the end of my nose. You are strong.... We rarely see people that look as good as you. You are doing really well. What is vasospasm? When the wall of an artery contracts and spasms, the artery reduces blood flow to that region of the brain, causing a second stroke.*

Fact: *Vasospasm is a common complication that may occur 5-10 days after a Subarachnoid hemorrhage (SAH) Re-bleeding and comas, and Hydrocephalus (Increased fluid and pressure around the brain) are the other dangers all can be fatal. Or cause major deficits.*

Hallucinations

Suddenly I was fixated on this gigantic floating bobbing eyeball that was hanging like a full moon staring at me. It was only one eye, not a pair. It had long lashes and was blinking.

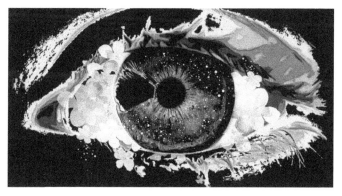

I watched it for a long time, and somehow we communicated. It did not scare me; I found it intriguing. Anything to break up the monotony. I was really interested in what it was expressing. It was very friendly. I was comforted in its presence. I was mesmerized. In walked the fun, young, and good-looking resident doctor. He was down to earth and had a good non-intimidating bedside manner. As he stood there and talked to me, I noticed a tree branch growing out of his head. It was rapidly growing, and the vines and branches were starting to spread out on the ceiling and walls. The leafy vines were beautiful. He told me the good news; they were going to take the tube out of my brain in a few days. I interrupted him and asked, "Do people ever see things in here?" He looked at me blankly and said like what? I told him about the tree growing out of his head and the floating eyeball. He said, "Yeah, all the time. They are called the ICU hallucinations." I continued to watch the branches spread out all over the room that were rooted in his head.

This image amazes me! It has so many of the components that my hallucinations had. **Delirium** *by Steve Munday.*

Somewhat distorted, the hospital was in my hallucinations
and my traveling in between the worlds.

In many worlds I traveled.

I saw many trees.

When I was about twelve years old, I had a near-death experience (NDE). I traveled and had the choice to stay or return. I was soaring high above gigantic trees. Trees have always had enormous power in my life. My first memory of animal communication and my belief that trees really do speak to us happened to me when I was about three years old. I was in my bed napping, and a tree and a squirrel spoke to me through the screen window of my bedroom on the second floor. That experience is still vivid in my mind. It has stuck with me.

> *Lines: Do people ever see things in here? There is a tree growing out of your head. I saw a big eyeball bobbing and floating and blinking at me. We get to take the tube out in a few days. Yes, people see things all the time in here. They are called ICU hallucinations.*

Doctor/nurse: *She is having hallucina-tions. She keeps talking about someone in the chair. Keeps pointing to the chair.*

Fact: *Traumatic Brain Injury patients go through a state of agitation and delirium. In the critically ill ICU delir-ium is common, including restlessness and agitation and hallucination. High doses of narcotics are also associated with delirium. Lack of sleep and being out of your natural element in a room without windows. Sleep deprivation and sensory overload combined; equip-ment noise, nurses, and lots of people coming and going. Loss of control of patients' lives. ICU psychosis often goes away in the morning or after sleep.*

My sister Monica often came to see me. Ironically, she was one of the only people I could tolerate. She brought me real coffee. She brought me a couple of blank journals for writing. Although I could not read or write at the time, it was a nice gesture. She knew my passion for writing. When I started this project, it was in these journals I began my writing. Her friend we had known from childhood, Colleen, sent a cool angel statue that hung and had a light-up candle feature. It hung in the room. Another Colleen, my trusted neighbor and friend caring for my dear cat, stopped by as well. I asked her to bring my mail and my checkbook. The fact that I was worried about paying my bills on time was a good sign that I was functioning at a rapid rate of recovery. Colleen, my neighbor and friend, is certified in Reiki healing. She performed some healing on me before she left.

I remember sitting up in my hospital bed. The struggle of thinking and multitasking and writing the correct amount on the correct check was my wake-up call. This was the first time I really realized just how badly my brain was damaged and what a struggle it was to do a simple task. I heard a nurse say she is getting really frustrated. This was confirmation that they were observing my behavior. Simple tasks exhausted me, things that we take for granted. A simple task feels as if you have just run a marathon. It hurts your brain, the frustration that it can't work as well as it used to, and you are suddenly aware of this. In the early stages of recovery, I felt this pain and frustration. Just looking for a pen or stamp was frustrating, difficult, and exhausting.

My handwriting, which is normally pretty nice, looked like a five-year-old wrote the check. An ICU nurse commented, "Now that's one I've never seen in here." I knew, even though this was too challenging for the moment, that I was way ahead of the game in recovery. I was writing checks and paying bills in my ICU bed. I was on a regimented pill plan. I think I was dozing off after my last dose and had forgotten that I told a doctor the university students could do research on me. Two very enthusiastic young women students entered my room. They pushed a TV on a cart and some weird device for me to rest my chin on. I was a total zombie from the drugs and the exhaustion of the day. I could barely keep my eyes open. They positioned my chin and had me follow their finger on the TV screen. Some weird cartoon was on, and I was drifting. They begged me to stay awake just a little longer. I have never in my life been so drugged and tired. I barely made it through. I fell asleep. My sister must have left as I drifted to sleep.

Lines: *Did you bring my checkbook? Do you want me to do Reiki? Yes, you can. Thanks for the Starbucks coffee. Stay awake just a little longer, just a little longer, and follow my fingers on the screen. Thanks for the journals. I love that angel!*

Doctor/nurse: *From Medical Press Release on EYE TRACKING RESEARCH The University of Minnesota is collaborating with Abbott and Hennepin.*

Hennepin County Medical Center has launched the nation's largest

*prospective study on concussion
and traumatic brain injury (TBI).*

Fact: *Neuro-fatigue is one of the most
debilitating consequences of a brain
injury. The energy of a whole day is
often consumed completely in a short
amount of time (about 2 hours).*

Every night in the early morning hours, a woman medical tech would wake me for an ultrasound of the blood vessels in my head. It was irritating and uncomfortable. She would always apologize. She wheeled this equipment over near me and then applied a cold gel to my temples. She would always say to be really still. *I need really good pictures of your blood vessels*. It was this invasion of personal space and it felt like she was hovering over me but she was, in fact, doing her job. Her face was in my face, and that invisible personal space boundary was crossed. I was always relieved when it was over.

The doctor came in and handed me a twenty-dollar bill for the research testing. I actually made some money in the ICU. It ended up being about eighty dollars after the course of my stay. I thanked him and said I missed making tips. He said we get to take the tube out today. This resident doctor was funny, and when he pulled the tube out of the ventricle in my brain, he distracted me and said EEEWWW, just think this was just inside your brain. He put it in a bag and said I have your brain goo in this bag. He kinda dangled it in front of me. I really appreciated his humor. He brushed the top of my head, I'm guessing with something anti-bacterial, and I winced in pain. It felt like a steel wool brush scraping.

I was getting more and more anxious to leave. I started breaking the rules. Shift notes summary. The patient was not using her call button before getting out of bed. I refused to listen to their orders, and they were sick of me. I was getting angry. I would say things like I can't take this any longer. I would constantly beep for everything and anything, a royal pain in the ass, and this is an understatement. I would yell from my bed. I went insane. The constant interruptions and constant stimulus of this place. I had been attached to a pole for a long time from a drain in my brain.... I felt free, and I was acting like it.

You have no idea how bad it is here I said. One sympathetic doctor understood me, as most of the nurses ignored me. He understood the need to be left alone. I started refusing to have my finger pricked and all the other jobs that I saw as unnecessary at the time. I was over the hump as far as I was concerned, and everyone became a nuisance or a bitch or an asshole. I had misplaced anger. I guess it was common in brain injury patients. Erratic behavior and outbursts of anger. One doctor, trying to empathize with me, admitted he, too, would go crazy in here. The delirium from lack of sleep and overstimulation and being out of your own element, hallucinations… that were real and not knowing what day it was or what time it was. Everything turned into a blur.… I could wake up at two in the afternoon and I had no idea what time it was. The clock on the wall meant nothing because time meant nothing when hours turned into days. I was awake at all different hours. My headaches were bad. The pain was excruciating and constant. All these drugs and still in pain. They gave me more meds, and I felt dizzy and off balance sitting up in bed.… I rested again.

> **Lines:** *I have your brain goo in the bag just think this was just in your brain. Here is a twenty dollar bill. Oh, yeah, thanks, I forgot I was making some money. Turn the heat down, turn the heat up, shut the door, goddammit, they sent some more meat in my lunch. I told the people I was vegetarian, unbelievable.*

> **Doctor/Nurse:** *Shift summary notes: Observed patient's behavior/anxious afraid apprehensive, verbalized anger, and frustration. Fact:*

The Drain not only eliminates fluid but monitors intracranial pressure (ICP) monitoring. A Temporary device allowing measurement and recording of intracranial pressure.

Fact: *Common complications following EVD insertion include hemorrhage, misplacement, dislodgement, blockage and infection, which could be further complicated by ventriculitis, meningitis, brain abscess, or subdural empyema.[6] These are associated with increased length of hospital stay, and morbidity.*

Ghost Dance

*My angels and the living dead sat,
walked, and wandered in a circular
motion as they repeatedly passed by
my bed with outstretched arms, almost
like they were tempting me or inviting me. They each gave me several
chances to leave. I continued to watch
them. I never felt that I was to join
them. They were good company. This
was the welcoming committee. They
wanted me to know they were there.*

*Persistent in their motion and very
ghost-like, all of them wore hospital
gowns like the one I had on. Their faces
were all dark and shadowed, without
eyes or features. I was trying to figure
out who they were. The one who was*

always sitting had a silhouette of a huge Beehive hairdo like the one my grandmother wore for years. She was always in the chair next to me and outstretched her arms from time to time.

I somehow made connections as I traveled in two worlds. I knew they were the living dead and my angels. I stretched in my mind to guess who the others might be. Some were dead relatives, and some were angelic. I would wake up, or some nurse would wake me, and my dead relatives and angels would phase out. I had a sense that they were always near, never far away."

—From my original essay.

They were near with outstretched arms and hands.

I then added this fitting quote by Janet Bettag:

In that nanosecond of enlightenment,
I knew that the human spirit
survives the death of the physical
body and I understood that my
wandering soul needed to get
back into its earthly habitat.

—Janet Bettag

Nabu and Spider were watching the dance, and Nabu instructed spider to not let me cross over. Spider told Nabu that I was clinging to this side, this world, and that the coils in my brain were secure and that I was out of danger. Spider then told Nabu that I recognized my grandmother and realized I was living in two worlds.

This image captures the motion and the feeling of my visitors. There was female and male energy, and the energy was ghostly, and cobwebs were everywhere in the movement. In my mind and in my room and it encased me. This is why I call the chapter *Ghost Dance*. I could hear the sound of slippers the ghosts wore on the hard cold hospital floors. There were details in the auditory hallucinations that surprised me. Even more so that I can remember both the visual and auditory to this day. The sounds and sights of my deceased visitors aroused my senses. Their faces were dark and shadowed, but sound and other senses that were present were enhanced as they visited. They were so close. This would look great in a documentary film. You could have a fast piece of chalk draw this image into being. These Dancing Ghosts!

The feeling… of motion and sounds, I remember. I felt them, and I heard them communicating non-verbally. The visitors passed by my bed, dancing. The motion I sensed. After a brain injury, senses get enhanced and diminished. Many of mine were enhanced. Aristotle was the first; he noted the five senses: touch, hearing, sight, smell and taste.

My grandparents, my beautiful grandmother with her beehive hairdo. She sat in the chair next to me in the ICU and stretched her arms out to me from time to time. Mostly I knew it was her because she appeared as the living dead with this hairdo. Without a doubt, I knew she was with me. Sitting very close. Her presence was incredibly strong. She was the only one who revealed herself or was allowed to.

She was always sitting in a chair and had a silhouette of a huge beehive hairdo like the one she wore when I was young. She would outstretch her arms from time to time. I somehow made connections as I traveled in two worlds. I stretched in my mind to guess who the others might be. I would wake up, or some nurse would wake me, and they would phase out. I had a sense that they were always near, never far away.

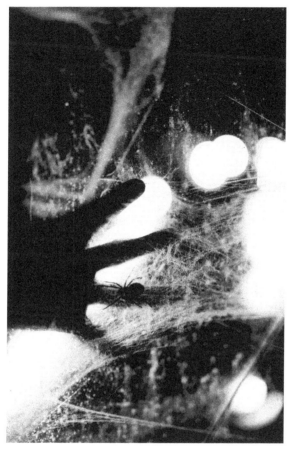

I woke up to an old boyfriend from many years gone by. He walked into the room. He always had a calming effect on me. We had texted a few weeks prior to my brain hemorrhage and talked about having coffee but never got together. I was able to get a text to him that I was in the ICU. He said, "I'll be there tomorrow." He also was like a dream or seemed as if his visit took place in another dimension. It was as if he, too, was a ghost.

Over the years, we would run into each other on occasion on the street, but many years had passed since our parting. Just a couple of months prior to my brain hemorrhage, we were connecting and messaging each other. It was in the ICU where we had that cup of coffee. His presence was peaceful, and he was always beautiful to me. He was like an angel. His presence could heal. I remember making eye contact with him, and it soothed me. It was powerful.

He is an excellent songwriter and poet. He brought me a gift of his poems that he printed and made into a book. He sat in a chair; we didn't say much of anything. He breezed out. If it wasn't for the book he left me, I would have always wondered and questioned if he was really there at all. Like the ghosts, he was there. Two years later, he told me he remembered pouring cream into my coffee, and I still have the book of poetry he left for me.

> *Lines:* She recognizes her grandmother, don't let her go. She doesn't want to, she is not leaving, and she is out of danger. The coils are secure in her brain. The majority of blood and fluid has drained. She enjoys astral travel, and she had an NDE as a young person. She is enjoying this between the worlds very much.

> *Doctor/nurse:* She is hallucinating today. She keeps saying someone is in the chair and pointing.

> *Fact:* Rebecca Valla, a psychiatrist in Winston-Salem, NC, who specializes in treating terminally ill patients, wrote in an email: "Those who are dying and seem to be in and out of this world and the "next" one often find their deceased loved ones present, and they

communicate with them. In many cases, the predeceased loved ones seem (to the dying person) to be aiding them in their 'transition' to the next world."

Homeward Bound / A Rough Departure

The team of neurosurgeon doctors and student doctors gathered around my bed again. They were all straight-faced with no expression. I scanned them with my eyes. I said, "there are so many of you." Their straight faces smiled, and a couple even let out a chuckle. They were checking me out. I felt like a Guinea pig or a lab rat.

> *From Medical Records: This is our woman who had a Basilar tip (area in the brain) aneurysm coiled. She is doing well. She has a mild visual field deficit but is otherwise intact. She has right visual field loss MRI confirms. Left optical infarct.*

I got back into my bed and in walked a physical therapist. She was cheerful and said do you want to take a walk with me? "Sure," I said. Weak and a bit shaky, we started walking the halls past the nurse's station. People were cheering me on, saying you're doing great. You're doing so well. You almost seem too good to be in the ICU. The PT was having me do very difficult things like walking with my head and looking up at the ceiling, combinations of challenging things after what I had suffered. I was weak and exhausted, but my drive and determination kept me going. I knew if I got through all this, I would be that much closer to being discharged. I got back into my bed and walked with the psychotherapist. She was eager to connect me with resources. I told her that I did not want any counseling. I just wanted drugs for pain and anxiety. I got a disgusted look from her. I did not like this woman.

Lines: Do you want to take a walk with me? You are doing really great. Can you walk and look up at the ceiling at the same time? How about some stairs? Can we try a few stairs? I don't want any counseling. I just want drugs for anxiety and pain.

Doctor/nurse: The patient refused psychiatric and psychological care and kept saying she did not want or need any.

Fact: Research shows us that ICU agitation and delirium can lead to combative behavior. A good doctor or nurse is trained in how to deal with this type of patient. There are step-by-step do's and don'ts.

Total chaos at the nurse's station, and there was a major delay in my discharge. There was a problem with the hospital pharmacy. They apparently did not have the very important medication in its proper dosing form on hand. It was to protect me from having seizures. It was taking hours, and I started raising hell. I was due for my last dose of pain medication. I received it still waiting for this hospital mishap to straighten out.

I was on a new floor and was becoming unpopular there. I was now torturing a whole new staff. I was rude and told the nurse what a horrible nurse he was. I kind of briskly walked after him, almost like a threat, and demanded my meds. There was no excuse for this. This was a hospital.

Someone contacted the staff from the ICU, and my friendly, nice resident doctor was called to the scene. He knew how fucked up this was. He was the troubleshooter, the only competent person dealing with this ridiculous situation (in my opinion). He said, "I'm going to have to pay a visit to the pharmacy." I said, "You mean you are going to kick some ass? They promised me hours ago this would be resolved." He promised me he would come up with a solution and even get them from another hospital or call Walgreens or something. I had faith in him. I said I'm going to get a cup of coffee and said they better be here when I get back. All my personal belongings were stacked and ready for me to grab and fly out of this place. I returned with my coffee. I had way too much to carry, and the exhaustion after this kind of brain injury is hardcore. I was doped on pain medication and very shaky and wobbly. The smart resident doctor was able to figure out that he could get the pills, but they were wrapped in foil rather than in a pill medication bottle. Just packaged differently. It took him to get this figured out after a whole team, plus a pharmacy, did not come up with plan B.

A nurse asked me do you have someone picking you up? I lied and said yes. It was protocol to have someone bring you home after an ordeal like this. She handed me all the meds, several bottles, and the foil-wrapped pills. She said to remember to read the instructions since they were not in a bottle. I just had a loose piece of paper with the dosing on it, a pharmacy printout, and the discharge papers.

Lines: *Where the fuck is my medication? Why is this taking so long? You said it would be ready in half an hour, you are an awful nurse!*

This is bullshit, this is a hospital, and you are out of this medication?

Doctor/nurse: *Pretty soon, I'm going to have to pay a visit to the pharmacy. They are out of one of your medications. I may have to get it from a different pharmacy or come up with a different plan. I'll make it happen. You mean you're gonna kick some ass!*

Fact: *From Nurse Bluff Blog: Being diagnosed with a serious illness, experiencing severe pain, and feeling frustrated about being confined in a hospital can make any patient easily agitated and angry. And when that patient starts to take his frustrations out on the entire healthcare team, you need to know exactly what to do to ease the situation.*

Photo of Me

Local writer thanks and apologizes to neurosurgery team and ICU nurses:

Dear neurosurgery team and ICU nurses at Hennepin Healthcare,

I was hospitalized on September 20, 2017, after suffering from a subarachnoid ruptured aneurysm and stroke. I spent two weeks in the ICU.

I really can't thank all of you enough!
I wish I knew each of your names!
I know that my personality in the
ICU was challenging and, at times,
extremely rude. I would like to take
this opportunity to thank you all for
the excellent care you provided...
and for putting up with me! Haha

I have continued to thrive and build
my strength pretty much back to
normal. However, as TBI survivors,
we are altered for life and never un-
scathed.... I hope you enjoy my story!

"Megan Bacigalupo, a local writer,
was rushed to HCMC after suffering
a subarachnoid ruptured aneurysm
and stroke last fall. Today, she is thriv-
ing and has regained her strength,
and grateful every day for the care
she received at Hennepin Healthcare,
particularly within the neurosurgery
team and the nurses in the ICU.

"However, she always had this nag-
ging feeling that she couldn't put behind her. Not only did she not thank
her caregivers at Hennepin for saving
her life and compassionately caring
for her for two weeks in the ICU, but
she felt bad that her behavior did not

reflect her actual self. She was rude and challenging to the nurses and other staff caring for her. The trauma that she was experiencing turned her into a person she was unfamiliar with and she didn't like her. Looking back, she always had this desire to apologize. Somehow, this would give her closure.

"The experts see different and erratic behaviors constantly and understand that in these traumatic situations, personalities change and patients aren't always at their best. It's understandable. It's expected, especially when it centers around trauma to the brain.

"But it mattered to Megan to express her gratitude and apologies.

"She documented her experience in *The Edge* where she is a contributing writer.

"Read 'In the Cobwebs of My Mind' by Megan Bacigalupo."[7]

The hospital featured my letter and wrote some of their own words and a link to my story[8] on their website/blog. It explains changes in personality after a traumatic brain injury (TBI).

7 From hospital blog https://bit.ly/3WRr6eN.

8 "In the Cobwebs of My Mind," https://bit.ly/42usk0O.

Final Exit / Final Act in Both Worlds

I had a purse and a shoulder bag. Some flowers that had been sent and a cup of coffee in my hand. I was weak. I started walking down the hallway. I was pushing myself. I knew my strength was wobbly. I lied to the staff and said I had a ride picking me up to go home. It was at this point I realized how fiercely independent I was. How much I looked forward to and longed to exit the hospital alone rather than with the drama of family chaos and dysfunction. They were glad to see me go. I did not thank anyone. I wanted to be free. I was weak and shaky and drugged. For a minute, out of the corner of my eye, I saw my dual self again, Horse. I thought he was not in the hospital, but he appeared to me as a symbol of freedom.

I found this in my search for images. It represents the duality of my character towards the end when the horse breaks free. One fades and one is strong. Yin/Yang. Yin Yang brought my story to life!

Nabu and Spider met me as I walked down the hall. I was not really going home alone. I was high on drugs and was unable to continue with the heavy load I was carrying. I unloaded the flowers at a different nurse's station. The three of us made it to the exit sign. As soon as I walked outside the hospital, standing at the automatic doors, the horse disappeared. He started at a fast trot pace, which then became a canter and finally a gallop. I heard the sound of his hooves fading. I looked over my shoulder to see him, but he was gone making his exit. I no longer needed him. My dual self broke free. It was just me.

I was strong enough now to release from my dual self... the sound of the fast trotting...

I love the final sketch of my dual self. He was free. I am free!

A sketch I did of a horse as I imagined the sounds and visuals for a show and on film. If I think about this, I can hear the echoes of the hooves on the surface of hospital floors sounding in my ears. It is a glorious sound!

Spider and Nabu still had a job to do.

The bus stop bench was not far from the sliding glass doors, so we exited. I got to the bench and sat down. The god of wisdom and writing, Nabu, sat on my right side and Spider on my left. We waited and rested until the bus came, and we got on the bus together. They were my escorts home.

This was the ending of the play that I envisioned.

When I was thinking of music for my show, a song by Joan Osborne called "One of Us," a song about god being on a bus making his way home, flooded into my mind. Joan Osborn also has a song called "Spider Web" on the same album, titled *Relish*. Both are funky and avant-garde, just as I imagined my show to be.

If my show or documentary comes to life like this book… I'll need to have these songs to really complete my vision. The songs, like my muses, chose this place to be. They, too, came to me like my original vision, only in an auditory way. These songs will blast at the end of the performance or in a film. The music will mix with horse hooves clipping along the cold hospital floors. As the horse exits the scene at the end and canters out the hospital's automatic sliding doors, I hear and see this now.

An incredible auditory and visual hallucination of a god named Nabu on the bus making his way home with a spider and my character.

What if God was one of us?
Just a slob like one of us
Just a stranger on the bus
Tryin' to make his way home?

Now you must listen to the music!

Joan Osborne, "One Of Us" https://youtu.be/aDdOnl0bHO4

Joan Osborne, "Spider web" https://www.youtube.com/watch?v=Txu8tss7aJ4

The writing part is done for now. Next, I will wait to see what **THIS** decides to shape up to be. This project has always moved and changed shape and form. So, a one-woman show, a documentary film, a short film or maybe a children's book?

Lastly, to all the survivors of traumatic brain injury, this is what my injured brain conjured up. I encourage you to experiment with what you might imagine or create. You are brave and courageous. You are alive. Tell your story.

Acknowledgments

I would like to thank the hard-working team at Calumet Editions: Ian Graham Leask, Gary R. Lindberg, Josh Weber, and Beth Williams for not only recognizing my story and wanting to take it on but, more importantly, making it come to pass. And to all the doctors and nurses that helped save my life. I am forever grateful to them at Hennepin County Medical Center (Hennepin Healthcare).

A special thanks to Tim Miejan, former Editor/ Publisher at *Edge* magazine. He was the first person to recognize and validate my writing. He helped me build a body of work and develop a style.

I thank my mother, Charleen, for believing in me and encouraging me.

I am so fortunate to have received the help and inspiration that came from Spider, Horse and Nabu. They were persistent as muses and stubborn until I moved forward with this project. Lastly, I would like to thank my mentor and friend, Bain Boehlke, for believing in me and my story and for his steadfast support throughout this enormous endeavor, which made it possible for me to see the light and press onward and upward.

About the Author

Megan Bacigalupo has been journaling and writing since childhood. She has been a contributing writer for *The Edge* magazine since 2012. Megan has a degree in Human Services and has worked in the restaurant business in Minneapolis on and off for decades. In 2017, she survived a near fatal brain hemorrhage while riding a bike. In early recovery, she immediately put the pen to paper and began recording her memories that documented her experience. This piece was titled *In the Cobwebs of My Mind* (the cobwebs refer to a cosmic space). This essay brought forth a vision that was impossible to ignore. It was this vision that set this book project into motion. From there it was all serendipity and synchronicity.

Since Megan's hemorrhagic stroke, she has had a couple articles published in national publications (*Reader's Digest* and *Human Events*). Megan is passionate about the ethical treatment of animals. She is intuitive and sensitive which makes her empathetic by nature. She considers herself a spiritual eclectic and a seeker of all things supernatural.

Printed in the USA
CPSIA information can be obtained
at www.ICGtesting.com
LVHW051934020823
754185LV00006B/76

9 781960 250872